FRONTIER
WITH A VE
THE EXECUTION OF
CLINTON DOTSON

JENNIE L. BROWN

For my father,
Jesse Oliver Dotson
(1896-1985)

and for my son,
Troy L. Couch

ACKNOWLEDGMENTS

In Montana, in 1982, library and newspaper office staff assisted me in locating newspaper accounts; courthouse staff photocopied trial transcripts for me. Not knowing I'd eventually write a book, I didn't record their names, but their gracious assistance is not forgotten.

In 1990, my cousin, Obern Dotson, furnished me with dated and documented newspaper accounts. I wish he were here today to see the result of his effort.

A few years later, I met Jo Dotson in West Union, West Virginia. She showed me a book that traced the Dotson family history from the Revolutionary War to the late twentieth century. I'm grateful for her time that day.

Charlotte Fleming, interested in her family's genealogy, contacted me in the mid-90s and offered to retype an early manuscript. Her work, too, contributed.

More recently, another cousin, Jack Frandsen, researched Captain Oliver Dotson. He supplied information about Clinton's early years in Deadwood, South Dakota.

In 2009, Nancy Taylor gave me an album that contained the last photo taken of Clinton. Her generosity is deeply appreciated.

The Missouri State Archives Staff, and staff at the Montana Historical Society Research Center, assisted me in tying up a few loose ends.

Every author needs a knowledgeable, skilled reader. I was fortunate to have the best of the best, Pamela Baughman Schmaltz, who not only read for me, but offered legal insight and useful suggestions. Thanks, Pam.

A special debt of gratitude is owed to Ernest C. Raymer, who designed the cover, untangled computer glitches, and restored photos and documents, Without his encouragement, support, and faith, I might have taken a long trip instead of sticking to the task.

TABLE OF CONTENTS

PART III–THE EXECUTIONS

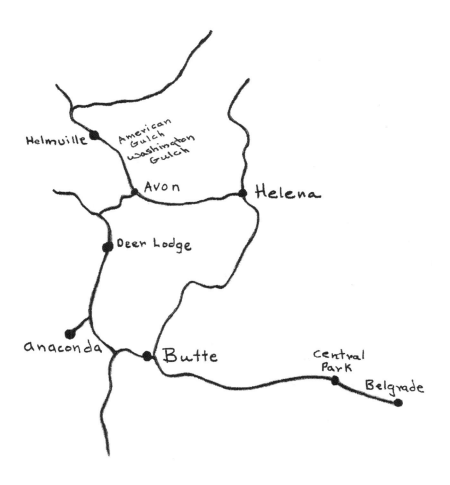

Southwestern Montana

*The price of anything is the amount of life you
exchange for it.*

~Henry David Thoreau

FOREWORD

I remember the day my father brought home a large stack of magazines; he'd bought every issue of that month's *Inside Detective* magazine available in our small town. I watched as he burned all but one copy. I have that copy today, and understand why my father didn't want his friends and neighbors to read the contents. In lurid detail, it describes the crime for which my grandfather, Clinton Dotson, was executed.

My father was a toddler at the time his father was hanged, and was the last to leave his mother's home, some twenty years later. I was born late in my father's life, an issue of his second marriage. The day he incinerated the magazines, my father began telling me Clinton's story. As I grew older, he gradually added more information. Curious, I broached the subject to my father's surviving brothers and sisters. Some were forthcoming; others still too stung by disgrace to comment. Later, I obtained original family documents and photographs.

From time to time, magazines that specialize in criminal cases publish a version of Clinton's story. Some of the accounts achieve a degree of accuracy, but others are fabricated, embellished, distorted, or exaggerated. Since much of the information available is from newspaper accounts, published when *yellow journalism* was at its height, this is somewhat understandable.

In 1982, I began researching Clinton's trials, and the circumstances surrounding his descent to the gallows. Since then,

I've gradually obtained more documentation. In the fall of 2009, a photo I'd long considered missing surfaced.

Clinton Dotson's story covers not one, but two trials. The first was his arrest and conviction for the murder of an old prospector. The second was for his alleged complicity in the death of his own father–my great-grandfather, Oliver Dotson.

It is not my objective to prove Clinton Dotson's innocence or guilt. Readers, like the jury who condemned him, must draw their own conclusions. What I can offer is an account based on fact. All wording in the interrogations, trial transcripts, documents, and newspaper accounts are unaltered. All names, dates, and relevant information originated in official records. Photos and copies of documents are from my collection, or from copies of the original official documents.

That said, the reader may ask how I know Clinton abhorred crowds, smoked a pipe, enjoyed coffee, or missed his wife. Although Clinton's probable thoughts–and those of his family– are my own invention, they are consistent with details supplied from family anecdotes, letters, and conversations with my father.

–Jennie L. Brown
February 2011

Part One

The First Murder

Chapter 1
The Capture
August 15, 1899

Clinton Dotson and his nephew, Charles Oliver Benson, finished setting up a crude, overnight camp several yards off the road leading northwest out of Belgrade, Montana. Their old spring wagon, one hind wheel tilted in at an angle, rested on a level spot of ground. The wagon's dashboard had long since vanished, and the tongue was spliced with a warped cottonwood pole. The frayed canvas cover sported a patch of black oilcloth. The team of bay geldings, Dan and Dick, now road-worn and spiritless, grazed on the late summer grasses.

Clinton stretched out in the shade of the wagon and fanned himself with his hat. He was gaunt from the hardship of living in the rough and not eating regularly or well. Charles, sometimes referred to by his middle name, Oliver, sat quietly nearby. He was unusually subdued for a young man who was restive by nature. The third traveler in the wagon, Ellis Persinger, a Missourian seeking greener fields in Montana, was at the general store in Central Park, a mile or so away, buying supplies for the evening meal. Clinton and Charles, relaxing in the shade, lulled by the hum of insects and the soft munching of the horses, were unaware they were enjoying their last few minutes of freedom.

Two days before, on Sunday, August 13, area law officers organized a frenzied search for the men and their wagon. Sheriff John Robinson, a deputy from Deer Lodge, Montana, was at the heart of the effort. He'd gathered enough information to indicate that Dotson, along with his nephew, would seek the sanctuary of Dotson's home in Whitewood, South Dakota. He posted an outer ring of guards to apprehend the men, regardless of what route they favored. Sheriff John Conley, of Anaconda, like Robinson, was taking no chances; he'd positioned himself so he could watch a road the men might take to reach South Dakota. Descriptions of the trio and their decrepit wagon were furnished to every sheriff and law officer in the area.

Clinton and Charles, sprawled in the wagon's shadow, were silent, each wrapped in his own thoughts. Benson, slow thinking, and often unable to articulate his ideas or fully comprehend the ideas of others, sat dumbly, halfheartedly flicking at the flies buzzing around the team's fresh droppings.

The young man had recently reached his majority, but in spite of a brief sojourn in the United States Navy before he deserted, remained unworldly and immature. He retained about him an unfinished appearance, as if an artist, outlining him in brief strokes, had never been inspired to fill in the sketch. His hair was light, dirty and unkempt. Had not his wispy beard and large, protruding ears been distracting, his blue eyes might have lent some substance to his face. He was of average height but slight of build. Next to his uncle, he looked soft and awkward.

Clinton was thin, but well muscled and graceful. He sat contemplatively, tamping tobacco into his pipe and waiting for Persinger to return with supplies. Soon, Clinton would start the coffee boiling over a makeshift campfire; no matter how hot the weather was, he enjoyed a steaming cup whenever he could get one.

Both men stirred and glanced up when they heard a rig approaching. The middle-aged traveler nodded pleasantly and passed by. Neither Clinton nor Charles felt any apprehension as the dust slowly settled.

Sheriff Robinson's heart was pounding from the encounter. He'd been shocked to suddenly come upon his prey, camped just a mile east of Central Park. He drove slowly until he was out of sight, forcing his shaking hands to keep the team at a steady pace. When he was at a safe remove, he urged the horses to cover the short distance to Belgrade swiftly. The fugitives had surprised him by camping casually along the roadside so early in the afternoon.

Robinson rushed into the telephone station at Belgrade where Sheriff Fransham from Bozeman was waiting for him. After a quick consultation, the two officers hired a fresh rig, alerted other law enforcement officials, and returned to the campsite. Benson and Dotson were still there–alone and unarmed.

Robinson quickly reined in the horses, bounded over the wheel of the rig, and leveled a shotgun at the startled men. "Hands up!" he shouted. Dotson complied immediately. Benson looked desperately about, then, on a second strong command, raised his arms as well.

Robinson kept his gun trained on the two men while the other officers located Ellis Persinger and arrested him as he left the general store. They brought him to the campsite and held all three men under close surveillance while they searched the wagon. The suspects were quiet and asked no questions. Persinger stood slightly apart, aloof from the others.

Later, an *Anaconda Standard* reporter described him as a "handsome man with clear blue eyes." His dark hair was sun bleached, and he wore an attractive, curly mustache. At thirty years of age, he stood slightly over six feet tall and weighed a strong 178 pounds.

The same reporter described Clinton as much smaller and older than he was, perhaps due to the liberal sprinkling of gray throughout his black hair. He was, at the time of the arrest, only thirty-eight years old.

While the trio of suspected criminals stood by, Sheriff Robinson and the other assembled officers began to explore the wagon. Clinton stood passively, displaying no emotion, as the officers ripped open an old mattress used for sleeping. Deep in the stuffing lay a gold watch. Sheriff Robinson held it up; it fit the description of the one taken from the body of Eugene Cullinane, an elderly miner found slain a week earlier. Also found in the wagon were a .38 caliber rifle, various valises, and cooking paraphernalia.

Sheriff Robinson searched the three men and duly recorded their possessions. Dotson carried $16.20 on his person; Benson possessed $2.30 and a flat key; Ellis Persinger also had a key, but only one cent in his pocket.

During the search the prisoners were silent, admitting only their correct identity. All three denied any knowledge of a crime or any wrongdoing.

Persinger, after giving his name, hastily claimed that he knew nothing of Dotson and Benson's activities. He said he'd met them in Helena and only traveled a short time with them. Surveying the men, Robinson came to a swift decision. Clinton's expression was stoic and noncommittal. Benson was obviously nervous and shaken; he kept glancing apprehensively at the officers, then at his uncle. Persinger was maintaining an air of outraged dignity and puzzlement. Robinson quickly surmised that, if separated, the furtive young man, Benson, would be the easiest to break. Persinger, also, might reveal all he knew to establish his alleged innocence. He could use those two to convict Dotson. Robinson acted decisively and took the three to Anaconda where he could interrogate them separately.

Chapter 2
Cullinane's Murder
August 8, 1899

Once in Anaconda, Deputy Sheriff John Robinson began questioning the three suspects. He had multiple reasons to believe that they'd murdered Cullinane, and only needed to confirm this belief to bring them to trial.

He'd first been contacted on August 10, when Sheriff John Conley of Anaconda responded to a wire from Michael Kiley, alerting him to the disappearance of Eugene Cullinane, a well-liked and gentle old miner who lived in American Gulch, near Helmville (Helmsville). American Gulch, like other nearby gulches–Nevada, Buffalo, California, and Washington–had been explored and worked by prospectors and miners since Washington J. Stapleton and two other prospectors discovered a new gold bar in a glittering creek.

The creek was named Washington; the gold bar was named Stapleton Bar. It was a rich discovery and many men, Stapleton included, made fortunes before abandoning it. The gold found there, although plentiful, was mined by a hydraulic system and required vast quantities of water. A company dug a thirteen-mile ditch from Nevada Creek to the gold bar, but charged such exorbitant rates for the water that most of the prospectors of the area became dispirited and left for easier pickings. In 1866, a post office was opened at Stapleton Bar and the name changed to Washington Gulch. The camp boasted one hotel, one store, two saloons, two livery stables and a stage stop. Helmville, fifteen miles northwest, provided another post office and a sheriff's office (Wolle 1963).

9

In 1899, Eugene Cullinane, like many elderly prospectors, lived in relative tranquility in one of the small cabins scattered throughout the area. He'd lived through the fever of the big strikes and now was content to enjoy the halcyon days that followed. Cullinane, as interested in the geology of the area as the possibility of finding a new deposit of gold, usually confined his prospecting to one-day excursions–leaving early in the morning with a pick and simple lunch. He would wander about the gulches, particularly during the warm summer months, content that he was living well, and confident that he'd provided for his relatives in the East.

Although rumored to have a fortune hidden on his person and in his cabin, in truth Eugene had deposited his wealth in a bank in Helena. It was neither a large amount, approximately $15,000, nor was it from gold he'd mined. Rather, he'd sold some mining claims years before and the money trickled in gradually as the buyers paid for the claims in installments. Eugene wasn't a poor man, but lived simply, shunning ostentation and high living. Perhaps his only vanity was a large gold watch that he wore proudly–a watch that was well known to anyone who was around Eugene for any time.

On the afternoon of August 8, a mild and peaceful Tuesday, Eugene Cullinane returned to his cabin from a short prospecting excursion. Preoccupied with his thoughts, he nonetheless hurried, eager to get home and feed and water his horse before the onset of evening. He entered a small glade, slightly less than a half mile from his cabin, where the trail narrowed as it snaked its way through close-growing trees and bushes. He slowed his pace to enjoy the sun-dappled silence of the bower.

Eugene never arrived home to tend his horse, and it was the frantic beast's whinnying that gave the first indication that something was wrong. John Mulholland, an elderly bachelor like Eugene, shared living quarters with the old man. He was fond of his roommate and respected the old miner for his generosity, and honesty. Although both took frequent trips to Helena, when together they found each other's company suitable and enjoyed an easy relationship.

Mulholland had left the cabin early in August and didn't return until the tenth. He heard Cullinane's horse neighing pitifully in the stable and hurried to check on the animal before walking to the cabin. When he opened the stable door, the creature stumbled out and rushed headlong to the water trough, drinking in great, painful gulps. Mulholland was shocked; Eugene always treated the beast kindly and would never deprive it of food or water. He rushed to the cabin, thinking Eugene might be ill or disabled, but found no trace of his presence. Panicked, he gave the alarm. He contacted thirteen of their friends and neighbors and began an organized search. Deputy Sheriff John Robinson traveled from Deer Lodge County; Deputy Sheriff Thomas Mullin of Helmville was alerted.

The search continued all that day, Thursday, to no avail. The team spread out over the entire northern part of the county, paying particular attention to American and Washington Gulches. Once, the men stopped when a dog began to howl plaintively, but continued when the dog stopped, unaware they had passed very close to Eugene's body.

Darkness closed in and they called off the search until the following morning. This time the officers developed a more systematic approach and again scoured the area. Sheriff Robinson found Eugene's body dumped in a dry gully, his face loosely covered with earth and leaves.

On September 5, 1899, a reporter for *The Anaconda Standard* postulated the following had taken place:

From the thicket at the side of the trail the bullet came. It entered the left side of his face, midway between nose and ear, ranged through the head, emerging at the base of the skull to the right of the spine. He fell to the ground, desperately wounded but not dead. In the long grass, he struggled desperately, rolling from side to side, striving with all his might to rise and face his cowardly assailants.

They beat him down with their weapons, wounding his arm in doing so, and then, as his back was momentarily turned to them, a second bullet was fired. It went through the body tearing its way through the organs, causing instant death and then lodging in the layers of flesh over the abdomen. To make sure of their deed, the murderers beat the gray head of the old man as he lay face down upon the sward. Deliberately they searched him.

It was a lonely place, a confederate was on watch and there was no chance of interruption. About the waist of the corpse they expected to find a belt lined with gold and notes. Fifteen thousand dollars was the sum they thought was in the belt. The clothing was rudely ripped apart and turned back over the head. No belt was there. In a pocket was found a rich gold watch, the case of 18-karat gold bearing the numbers 1125; the works bore the number 2548000. In other pockets a small sum, somewhere between $10 and $15 was found. This was the reward of the crime.

Two men lifted the bleeding and mutilated body, wrapped it loosely in a piece of canvas and bore it about 60 feet away to a little dry gully where, last spring, had spread a brook. They dumped their burden into the gully, covered the face with earth and brush and leaves, piled an inch or so of earth upon the body, and left it.

If the reporter's fanciful description didn't convince the public of the severity of the crime, his final comments effectively prepared them for the forthcoming trial:

Possibly some of these days Deer Lodge County may see a triple hanging. If so, the people of Washington Gulch will feel the death of their loved friend and neighbor has been revenged. Until that hanging takes place they will believe

12

the gallows has been cheated and that the courts are a mockery.

The article appeared over a month before the trial of Clinton Dotson began and before a jury was picked. Public opinion, which had simmered since August 10, fueled by the newspapers and grieving friends of Eugene Cullinane, was now aflame. The good citizens of the area clamored for fast action.

Chapter 3
The Investigation
August 1899

Deputy Sheriff Robinson's interrogation of Clinton proved vastly disappointing, made even more so by his inability to evoke emotion or fear in the prisoner. Robinson made known to Dotson there was a strong case against him, but the sober-faced, weary man obstinately denied any knowledge of the crime.

Robinson's first move was to inform Clinton that a longtime friend and close companion of Eugene Cullinane, named John Chadwick, had come forth and accused him. Chadwick had related to the law officers, before the capture of the three men, that Clinton Dotson and Charles Oliver Benson had approached him with a proposition to kill Cullinane for his money.

Dotson had allegedly insisted to Chadwick that he *knew* Cullinane kept thousands of dollars on his person. Their plan was for Chadwick to watch Cullinane's movements and inform them when the time was ripe to rob the old man. Afraid of Dotson, Chadwick said he'd made a tentative promise that he would join them. Satisfied with his pretense, they left and Chadwick immediately sent word to Cullinane to warn him of the plot that endangered him. Unfortunately for Eugene Cullinane, the man Chadwick chose to carry the message didn't take the elderly Chadwick seriously.

Many old men, tucked away in small cabins in the mining gulches, were living on dreams of glories past; of days when they were important men within the mining community; of the times when they easily carried small fortunes of gold dust, tightly wrapped, in bags secreted on their bodies. In their minds they recalled the time when a sharp eye and a ready firearm were

14

necessary for survival whenever a man stepped outside his dwelling.

Younger men, like Chadwick's messenger, thought the old miners exaggerated. The particular man Chadwick entrusted with the warning for Cullinane had practical considerations on his mind, and had no time to worry about an old man's hallucinations. Privately, he thought Chadwick was fast becoming senile. He never delivered the message.

Sheriff Robinson wasn't so quick to dismiss Chadwick. When the wintry old prospector accused Clinton Dotson and his nephew, the sheriff listened and gave credence to the claim. Robinson thought there was a good chance of the story being true, particularly after Chadwick pointed out that the two men made the trip from the Black Hills to Washington and American Gulches frequently, ostensibly to visit Clinton's aging father, Oliver, another old man settled into a solitary life of occasional prospecting.

Chadwick hinted malignantly that whenever Oliver's son and grandson departed from the area, sluice box robberies were discovered. He said the robberies always coincided with their visits. He carefully characterized the battered spring wagon they traveled in, and gave detailed descriptions of the lean, older man and his vacant-faced nephew.

Robinson pressed him for more details about the conspiracy. Chadwick, delighted to be in the thick of an important investigation, said Clinton had planned to stay in Helena long enough to establish a presence there for an alibi, then return to secretly rob the old man and depart for the relative safety of his home in South Dakota.

Shortly after talking with Chadwick, and before arresting Clinton and his companions, Sheriff Robinson had arrested Clinton's father, Oliver Dotson, and Clinton's brother-in-law, Edward Cachelin, plus two other men; he claimed he believed the four to be involved in the conspiracy. The sheriff then went to great lengths to keep the identities of these men secret, publishing their names as John Oleson, John O'Brien, Dan Dee, and William Jones. The only cause Robinson gave for suspecting them was the fact they had been prospecting nearby. Robinson's reasoning at this time seems strange and somewhat fragmented for a trained, experienced law officer.

He talked with John Chadwick on August 10, the day Cullinane's body was discovered, and acknowledged the old man's suspicions. He'd then reported the conversation to Sheriff John Conley. Conley resembled Grover Cleveland, due to the pouches under his eyes, his long, full cheeks, and his walrus mustache. Both his appearance and his demeanor commanded respect. Conley told Robinson to send Chadwick to Anaconda for further questioning.

After interviewing Chadwick, Conley traveled to American Gulch to see the murder scene for himself. Following his trip, an inquest was ordered: the verdict stated Cullinane met his "death at unknown hands."

The following day, August 11, 1899, the Justice Court in Anaconda Territory, Deer Lodge County, issued a warrant of arrest that authorized Joseph Daly to arrest the suspects. It was originally written out for Oliver Dotson, C. O. Benson, and John Doe.

At this time, the officers were aware that the three men were traveling in an old wagon. They further believed, on the strength of Chadwick's accusation and the physical evidence, Dotson, Benson and the *John Doe* were the culprits. Yet, Robinson arrested the other four men and jailed them under pseudonyms. He seemed to think they, too, were guilty and hoped that one of them might turn state's evidence. One can only deduce that, unsure of Chadwick's information, he was trying to throw up a smoke screen–or he seriously believed that all seven men had conspired to rob and murder one helpless old miner.

He soon realized the injudiciousness of arresting the four men who had been mining nearby, and released them on $600.00 bail each. Ed Cachelin put up the money for his aged father-in-law, Oliver. Oliver, respectfully called Captain Dotson since his years on the Missouri River, was a staunch old prospector who had worked hard at honest endeavor for most of his nearly seventy years. Cachelin, his son-in-law, was a respected South

Dakota business man and community leader. William Glover and Gabriel Hilderbrand were unlikely candidates as well. After they were released, the search for Clinton, Benson and Persinger intensified.

Sheriff Robinson said that Hilderbrand, before his release, had revealed information to the officers that was incriminating to Clinton Dotson and his traveling companions, but the exact nature of the information was never made public. It was noted, however, that Robinson corrected the arrest warrant to read Clinton Dotson, C. O. Benson and Ellis Persinger after conferring with Hilderbrand.

In spite of the arrest of the wrong men initially, Robinson finally believed he had the correct three criminals in hand. He took Dotson and Persinger to the penitentiary at Deer Lodge for safe keeping. It became apparent to Robinson that Dotson wouldn't vary his story, even when confronted with the most damning evidence–the gold watch belonging to Cullinane. He'd further challenged Clinton with other physical evidence. At the scene of the crime, Robinson had found fresh tracks made by a wagon with a damaged wheel, turned inward and leaving a scalloped impression in the soft dirt of the roadway. Clinton's wagon displayed the same defect.

Even more incriminating were footprints found at the scene of the murder. The tracks near the old miner's body indicated that, while one of the killers had worn a broad soled shoe, the other had worn a slender, pointed-toe shoe. Dotson, ever careful about his appearance, remained stony faced when Robinson told him that his unusual, pointed-toe shoe fit the impression found at the makeshift grave site. Clinton's vanity in wearing a shoe more suited to the environs frequented by an eastern business man or a river boat gambler, than to the rough gulches of Montana, seemed to place him firmly at the murder scene. Still, Dotson maintained a stolid disregard for the evidence and insisted he knew nothing of the crime.

The interrogation of Ellis Persinger provided Robinson with little to go on. It seemed at times the man's memory was highly defective to the point that he occasionally claimed to have no recall of his past life. This was, no doubt, selective amnesia as he'd left a lifetime of friends and relatives in Missouri, as well as a wife and three children.

Persinger, disappointed with the slow recovery of his home state after the Civil War, had struck out for the West and a chance to find wealth. Whether by chance or by choice, he found himself in Montana in the company of Dotson and Benson. Now, he seemed determined to keep his predicament from his acquaintances and loved ones in Pattonsburg, Missouri. He maintained he was an innocent bystander to the entire affair.

Disgusted, Robinson concentrated his efforts on young Benson, who had deliberately been retained in the county jail, effectively separated from the counsel of his uncle. Witnesses began coming forth and stating they had seen the three men, in the distinctive old wagon, on the road leading to and from the scene of the killing. Benson, either from fear of, or cooperation with, the officers, volunteered a statement on August 16, 1899 in which he tried to maintain his and Clinton's innocence.

Chapter 4
Benson Interrogated
August 16, 1899

Charles Oliver Benson was sweating profusely in the late August heat. The sheriff's office wasn't commodious, and Charles sat hunched on a wooden chair, shifting uncomfortably while trying to avoid the eyes of the men grouped near him. He repeatedly rubbed his left hand across his brow, wiping the moisture away. He'd tucked both feet as far under the chair as the bottom rung would allow. He knew that footprints had been found at the scene, and he tried to hide his shoes, as if someone would snatch them away from him.

After being sure the stenographer's pen was in place, County Attorney J. H. Duffy of Deer Lodge, Montana, straddled a chair directly in front of Benson and put forth his first question.

Q. Can you be particular as to the day of the week you and him left Helena for the purpose of going east? Figure in your own mind exactly back if you can.

A. I think it was the 11th. I am not sure.

Q. What time did you get into Helena?

A. We got there on Tuesday, next day after we started.

Q. How many days did you stay in Helena?

A. We was there about two weeks.

Q. Were you in Helena all this time? Was you there for two weeks?

A. We was there about that time.

Q. Had you driven from Washington Gulch to Helena?

A. Yes sir.

Q. Where was he, Dotson, on the nights of the 5th, 6th and 7th of this month?

A. I don't know. I guess he was down in the wagon.

Q. Where were you on the nights of the 5th, 6th and 7th?

A. I was up town.

Q. You don't know whether or not you slept with him these nights?

A. No sir.

Q. These particular nights you don't know whether or not you slept in this wagon or not?

A. No sir.

Q. What kind of gun did he have?

A. He had a rifle.

Q. What caliber was it, do you know?

A. He had a .38 caliber rifle.

Q. Just a .38?

A. I think that's what it was.

Q. How many cartridges did it explode?

A. I don't know.

Q. Did he have it when he came to Washington Gulch?

A. He had it when he came to Washington Gulch.

Slowly, the official worked on Benson to make him establish Clinton Dotson's exact whereabouts. Benson repeatedly answered, "I don't recollect," or "I don't remember," when asked to name the date or the day the party had left Helena. Duffy then changed tactics abruptly to gain evidence concerning Eugene Cullinane's gold watch. It was the State's prime piece of evidence.

Q. How did you keep track of time?

A. By a clock.

Q. You had no other time pieces?

A. No sir.

Q. Did Dotson have a gold watch on him?

A. No sir.

Q. Did you ever see him with a gold watch?

A. I never seen him with a gold watch.

Swiftly, the questions were switched back to the progress the men had made in the old wagon. Benson cowered in the chair, becoming more dazed as he tried to remember what he'd just told them.

Q. After you broke camp this side of Beaver about 8 o'clock in the morning, where did you go from that point?
A. I don't think we stopped here in town at all.
Q. Where did you next camp?
A. Along side of the road.
Q. Railroad?
A. No sir, wagon road.

Patiently, they led the fumbling Benson through the trip. They learned the men's ultimate destination had been South Dakota. Benson had begun to relax somewhat until he was asked bluntly:

Q. When did you first observe the presence of this watch?

It startled Benson to see Eugene Cullinane's gold watch thrust in front of him. He instinctively pulled back and dropped his eyes to his lap. Pushing the particular watch forward, the interrogator continued sharply.

Q. When?
A. I seen the tall fellow with it down at camp.

Benson was referring to Persinger, who he avoided calling by name. In his conversation, he would identify Ellis Persinger as the "other fellow" or the "one who said he came from Missouri." Benson pretended to know little about him.

Q. Where did the tall fellow say he got it?
A. He said he bought it from a man at the wagon.

Q. At what point was the wagon then?
A. At Central Park.
Q. After you left Helena?
A. Yes sir.
Q. Was it there you first saw this watch?
A. That's where I first saw it.
Q. You don't know how long that watch was there?
A. No sir.

Benson was perspiring heavily now, but he seemed oblivious to the rivulets running down his temple and soaking into his shirt collar. Duffy leaned back and conversationally referred to a gold pouch.

Q. When did you first see that big pouch to carry gold?
A. That was in the wagon since we started from Helena.
Q. It was in the wagon before you left Washington Gulch?
A. Yes sir.
Q. Who put it there?
A. I don't know.
Q. Whose was it?
A. I got it from Hilderbrand.
Q. How long before you left Washington Gulch?
A. I don't know. I don't remember just how long it was.
Q. Were you with Dotson and this other fellow all the time?

At this point, Benson had an idea penetrate the confusion. A deviation from the story he'd rehearsed might absolve him from blame. He then tried to establish his absence from the others.

A. No sir.
Q. How did you get–come to get–separated from him?
A. I was up town.
Q. Whereabouts up town was you?
A. I was running around to different places.
Q. How far is Central Park from Helena?
A. In the outskirts of town.

Q. Did it take you all evening to go from Helena to Central Park?

Benson hesitated and looked up inquiringly. He was becoming perplexed and realized he didn't know the geography of the area well. His questioner pressed on, sensing an advantage.

Q. You told me just a minute ago that you, this big fellow with the white hat, and Dotson were camped at night at Central Park.
A. Yes sir.
Q. Where was you when the trade was made?
A. I was up town.
Q. Was Dotson present when the trade was made for the watch?
A. I think he was.
Q. You didn't see this trade made?
A. No sir, they was talking about it.
Q. Who was talking about it?
A. Ellis and the other fellow.

Duffy had won a small point, but Benson was totally unaware of it: Benson now was acknowledging Ellis Persinger by his first name, rather than pretending not to know him other than as a "fellow from Missouri." As the hot afternoon wore on, Duffy calmly continued, apparently impervious to the stifling atmosphere.

Q. Where did this fellow get the watch?
A. I think he bought it from a stranger.
Q. Didn't you say a minute ago you didn't know where this fellow got the watch?
A. No sir.
Q. You didn't say that?

Giving Benson no time to collect himself, the County Attorney pressed his advantage.

Q. Was you present when the watch was bought?
A. No sir.
Q. When was you present?
A. It was the night before we left.
Q. That's the night before you left Central Park to go east?
A. Yes sir.
Q. At that time there was you, Dotson, and this big white-headed fellow?
A. Yes.

Duffy noted with satisfaction that Benson was now answering almost automatically, not noticing the subtle change in phrasing from "white hatted" to "white headed." The heat and the lengthy, monotonous questioning was wearing the shallow young man down to where he no longer thought before he answered.

Q. Now will you describe this man you met the night before?
A. He was a short, heavyset fellow.
Q. Where did he say he got the watch?
A. He didn't say.
Q. Was you there when he first came to your camp?
A. No sir, I was not there.
Q. Was you there when they were talking about selling it?
A. No sir.
Q. Didn't you say that you were there when this man was talking about it?
A. I came there just after it was bought.
Q. Then you were not present at any time before it was actually bought?
A. No sir.
Q. Then the first you knew of that transaction was when it was—when the watch was actually bought?
A. Yes sir.
Q. If you were present didn't you know how much money he paid for it?
A. Four dollars is what he told me.
Q. Who told you?

A. Ellis.

Q. You were present you say?

A. I was there but I was not paying attention to him.

Duffy continued, extracting from Benson the statement that it didn't seem unusual that a man would sell a gold watch for $4.00. Then, leaning forward, Duffy stated brusquely, "The transaction never took place at all."

Benson, stricken, replied weakly, "I heard that they bought it for $4.00."

Switching his line of questioning, Duffy adopted an affable manner and began asking Benson about the men's evening meal, trying to learn if the "short, heavy man" had eaten with them that evening. The depth of Benson's inability to think coherently became evident in his answers. He began calling his uncle by his last name and the drifter from Missouri by his first name. When he was told, "We know you are lying about this watch. We have got that evidence in our possession," Benson seemed to shrink into himself.

He was lost without his uncle to guide him. He knew he'd varied his story, but couldn't remember how often or in what direction. The questioners weren't giving him time to think back and recall exactly what he'd said. The oppressive heat of the afternoon closed in tighter than ever, nearly suffocating the young man. He tuned in and out to the voice pressing him for answers. Sometimes he simply said he didn't know or didn't remember, at other time he made an effort to supply an answer that would satisfy them.

During the next series of questions, Duffy and the men present managed to draw the admission from Benson that he didn't know if Clinton Dotson had ever been away from the wagon or not. He stated he didn't know Dotson's whereabouts at all times, but the man from Missouri had been with Dotson for approximately two weeks in Helena, and they might have both been absent from the wagon for a day or two. Also, they had gone down to John Chadwick's one day and Dotson had talked with Chadwick, but he didn't know what they talked about. He admitted he'd hollered from his cell the night before they were separated and talked to his uncle, kept in another cell nearby.

Duffy focused on the alleged conversation, trying to show that Benson had been instructed by his uncle to deny knowledge of the watch or crime.

Q. Why did you come to talk with him (Dotson)?
A. I hollered and asked him.
Q. Why did you holler and ask him then if you were innocent of any knowledge in the matter?
A. I don't know.
Q. While you were over in the Bozeman jail you hollered and asked him about this watch?
A. I didn't holler! I asked him.

Duffy abruptly switched to asking Benson about his previous experiences in the Navy. Benson had enlisted in the Navy in Philadelphia and was assigned to the vessel, ESSEX, under the command of Captain Strong. He said he thought he'd enlisted in 1896 and was in for about two years. When asked where he was discharged, he defensively answered that he wasn't but had "gone ashore" at Tampa Bay, Florida. When pressed, he admitted he'd deserted. He insisted he'd deserted in 1897, although he wasn't sure of the month.

When urged to remember more exactly, he decided that since he'd served two years, maybe it was 1895 when he enlisted. From Tampa Bay, he'd traveled to some town, the name of which he couldn't recall; he thought it might have been in Pennsylvania, perhaps Pittsburgh.

Painfully, Duffy led the young man through the tangled web of his memory until he ascertained that Benson had gone first to Jacksonville, then Pittsburgh, hence on to Kansas City and through Indian territory until he came to Montana. As time wore on, Charles hesitated longer and longer before answering.

Q. Can you explain to me why you have to think of those answers so long?

A. I forgot the names of the places.

Then, abruptly, Duffy asked the question Benson was dreading, the question that could directly implicate him.

Q. What kind of shoes did you wear? Square toes or pointed?
A. Round toes.
Q. What size were they?
A. I think they were sevens.
Q. What size do you generally wear?
A. I generally wear sixes or sevens.
Q. Do you run them down on the heel on either side?

Benson pushed his feet back under the rung until it cut painfully into his ankles and the chair was in danger of tipping forward.

Q. Do you run the heels down at the sides?
A. Once in a while.
Q. What would you have to say if the testimony showed that tracks were found where this body was found that were made by a pointed shoe–six or seven in size–and run down at the right side of the heel?
A. I would say they wasn't mine.

It was apparent the exhausted Benson could offer nothing that would shed any further light on the matter. Duffy motioned for the stenographer to type the material quickly so Benson's signature could be affixed. The next day Benson signed his statement in the presence of J. H. Duffy, County Attorney, and three other witnesses. He neither read nor showed any interest in the document. Seven days later he would break completely and furnish a damning confession that would seal his uncle's fate.

Chapter 5
Clinton
August 16, 1899

While young Benson was sweating through the interrogation, Clinton sat quietly in his cell. The prison guard had returned Clinton's pipe and tobacco to him, and, as he smoked, Clinton found himself worrying about his team of horses. Across from him, Persinger paced nervously back and forth in his cell, occasionally calling out an accusation or entreating the older man to "Get me out of this."

Mostly Clinton ignored him, thinking about Dan and Dick, his bay horses. He worried the sheriff had confiscated them and would probably keep them. He knew Dan wasn't worth much, he was getting old; Dick, on the other hand, was still strong and lively and had some good years left. The children loved them. When he came home from his frequent travels, the older boys would spend long afternoons brushing the coats of the team horses, especially Dick's whose light, reddish-brown color gleamed like polished copper from their ministrations.

Clinton closed his eyes, remembering his wife yelling at them in a mixture of English and German, telling them it was nothing but a team of work horses, not race horses. Milking the cow was more important, and she couldn't cook supper if one of the lazy *schafkopf* wouldn't get some kindling split for the stove.

Even his youngest son, Jesse, had tried to handle Dan and Dick. Clinton felt a pang of remorse, remembering the last time he was home and the whipping he'd given Jesse. There was a deep well on his homestead near White Wood, and he and Mary had repeatedly warned the children to be careful around it. The well plunged far into the earth, and would be sure death for a child who slipped and fell to its depths.

The last time Clinton was home, Jesse had led Dan to the well, and tied the old workhorse's reins to the railing. Dan instinctively shied away, and the weak railing tore loose. Jesse, leaning against the railing, went sprawling across the gaping mouth of the well. Clinton saw it happen, and raced breathlessly to save his son, barely managing to grab the boy before he slipped into the depths. Reacting from fear and anger he'd beaten the boy until Mary stopped him.

He was too hard on his boys, he thought. Mary was right; he needed to be gentler. He would be if he got out of this prison and home again. Mary must be sick with worry; she was expecting him soon and he didn't think anyone had told her yet that he was in jail, held on suspicion of murder. She would be out of money by now, too; he'd only been able to leave her a few dollars when he was home last. Clinton puffed miserably on his pipe. What would happen to his babies?

Clinton's life had always been affected by babies. This fifth child in a family of eleven would father nine children of his own by the time he was thirty-eight years old. Only a few years of his life, from his late teens to his early twenties, had been free from the needs and demands of infants.

Clinton's father, Oliver Dotson, was a fourth generation American, descended from one of seven brothers who came from England in the early 1700s. In 1852, when he twenty-two years old, Oliver married Miss Sarah Flemings of Arnold's Creek, Doddridge County, West Virginia. He and Sarah, four years his junior, spent much of their married life following Oliver's quest for riches. Sarah soon learned that life with Oliver was one of constant motion and childbearing; her babies came quickly and ceaselessly.

Their first child, Susan Columbia, was born on July 1, 1853. She acquired a sister in July of 1854 and a brother on Valentine's Day, 1856. When the third child died in infancy, Oliver packed his wife and two surviving daughters into a wagon and left West Virginia to find their fortune somewhere in the West.

For a while they stopped in Omaha, Nebraska, but the lure of a better opportunity called to Oliver. The family traveled to Colorado, this time in a covered wagon making its painful way along the Overland Trail. Oliver and his twenty-three-year-old wife settled temporarily in Colorado. Although he engaged in some prospecting, Oliver found a better income in working with the surveyors who were laying out the future city of Denver. At one point he found profit in producing the stakes used by the crews; however, he failed to make his fortune in Colorado. With a lust for gold firmly entrenched by then, he moved his family to yet another mining area.

This time, they settled into a small shack in Alder Gulch, Montana. Shortly thereafter, Sarah gave birth to her fourth child, a boy. This child had barely reached the toddler stage when she again labored to give Oliver a son. This boy, her fifth child and second living son, was born on October 10, 1860. She named him Joseph Clinton Dotson.

Clinton was only able to enjoy the status of being the youngest child for seventeen months before Sarah gave birth to another son After that, Clinton received very little individual attention from his mother, preoccupied with the latest baby at her breast. He received even less from his restless and ambitious father.

When he was two, the family moved to Leadville, Colorado, then to a series of Colorado mining camps. When he was four years old, the family was back in Alder Gulch. When he was five years old, his father settled his family briefly in Fort Benton, Montana.

In that year, 1865, Fort Benton played host to hundreds of people, scores of oxen, horses, draft animals, domestic animals, and thousands of tons of supplies and freight destined for the gold mining towns surrounding Helena. Optimistic prospectors poured into the area, followed closely by entrepreneurs hoping to make their fortunes off the miners. The towns teemed with adventurers, criminals, and riffraff of every description,

It is strange that Oliver chose to leave Fort Benton, a thriving region of bonanzas and gold camps to move his family to the flat plains of Nebraska; however, once he decided to do so, he built a small boat to transport his family, by way of the Missouri River, to the small village of DeSota, Nebraska, north of Omaha. The trip to DeSota was as harrowing as living in the muddy, ramshackle boom towns had been.

The Missouri River, seen as an avenue to the wealth of the West, was also treacherous: muddy, churning, and replete with snags, sand bars, rocks, shoals, and constantly shifting banks. To travel in a small, homemade boat, with his wife and young children aboard, testified to both Oliver's courage and the fatalistic approach to life so commonly found in the west of the 1860s.

Oliver took his family east along the Canadian border before dropping down through the Dakota Territory into Nebraska. Clinton, with a young boy's enthusiasm, thrilled to the danger of passing over the seething Drowned Man Rapids a hundred miles below Fort Benton and watching his father navigate the hazardous shoals of Cow Island, 30 miles farther down the river.

The shoreline provided sights to enchant the boy. He saw herds of buffalo so dense on the plains above Fort Berthold that the land looked like a moving black wave. Indians roamed the shoreline waiting for foolhardy boats to anchor in a lonely place.

Once settled in DeSota, Oliver bought up timber tracks and manufactured barges. His success in moving his family, and his experience building barges, inspired Oliver to look to the Missouri for a new career. He spent the next ten years working on *The Lady Grace* and *The Sunset*, steamboats that hauled wood from the upper to the lower river during the peak logging days of 1866 to 1876. It was on the river that he earned the title Captain Dotson: an appellation that stuck with him until his death.

Back in DeSota, it was a harsh life for Sarah and her children. In late April 1866, her oldest daughter, Susan Columbia, wrote to her uncle Eli (Sarah's brother). Her letter reflects the hardship and loneliness of life in the West, and her concern for West Virginia relatives in the aftermath of the Civil war.

*d your letter of April 12 and it gave us joy to hear
again. We had give out hope of ever getting a letter
ꓕᵣₒₘ you again. Mother wants to see you and the children
bad Uncle Eli. I want you to write and tell me how many
battles you were in. When you write tell me if Wesley got help
from the war or not and if he got hurt or not. Oh, uncle, you
do not know how people lives and dies here. When you write
I want you to tell me who was killed in the war that we have
known. Mother has a cow. She was offered 200 dollars for
her. Eggs are worth 2 dollars and 20 cents a dozen. We bot a
sack of flour for 23 dollars and we thot it was very cheap. We
just eat one sack of flour every two weeks. The snow has been
2 feet deep here . . . Mother said that paper was getting
scarse so that you couldn't write.*

When Clinton was eight years old, his mother, Sarah, visited
West Virginia. She'd just lost her latest baby, a girl named Molly,
and buried her in the DeSota burial ground. She was pregnant
again when she began her journey to her people's home in the
countryside of West Virginia. She stayed a year, leaving the older
children in DeSota to fend for themselves when Oliver was
absent–which was most of the time. Her ninth child was born at
the farm home of Oliver's father, John Dotson, in November
1868.

After years of rough living, Sarah had joyfully anticipated the
homecoming, longing for the level of civility she remembered.
The visit, however, was fraught with disappointment. The Civil
War had made many changes: friends and relatives, fighting on
the side of the Confederacy, had disappeared or been killed;
deprivation had robbed the people of their will and many were
steeped in apathy and depression. Conditions were mean and a
general air of hopelessness and helplessness prevailed.

While she was away, her fifteen-year-old daughter, Susan,
had married. Her other daughter, Virginia, fourteen, followed suit
shortly thereafter and married Charles Benson, a cabin boy on
her father's steamer. (It would be the son of Virginia and Charles'
union who would–in August of 1899–accompany his uncle,

Clinton, on a venture that ended the life of an aged miner and began Clinton's descent to the gallows.)

When Sarah returned at the end of the year with her latest baby, she took up life where she'd left it, eventually producing children numbers ten and eleven.

In the meantime, Clinton turned to his father for companionship and began learning the river—a heavy charge for a young boy. It was on the river that he learned the history of his favorite steamboat, *The Lady Grace*. Built in Madison, Indiana, she carried 387 tons "burthen" and boasted three high-pressured boilers, twenty staterooms, forty berths for cabin passengers, and cramped quarters for Captain Dotson.

The glamour of steam boating on the Missouri made the dangerous, grueling work and monotony worthwhile to Clinton. At every gathering, river men told and retold stories of famous storms, appalling wrecks, and desperate gambles—heady tales to a young boy. Like every child, he named his heroes, and a Captain Grant Marsh was one of them. Clinton thrilled to hear of the ten steamers Captain Grant commanded. He would, as an adult, talk often about the *Far West*, the most famous of Marsh's vessels, and knew by heart the story of Grant Marsh taking the *Far West* into Sioux Country in 1876. He told his sons of the memorable meeting aboard the vessel between General Custer, General Terry, and General Gibbons before Custer's disastrous last battle.

Clinton recounted the exploits of the *Ida Stockdale* when her crew fought off a violent Indian attack in 1868. There were scores of steamboats on the river in the 1860s and 1870s; small, crude boats competed with larger, more luxurious boats to capture the traveler's dollar. They plied the river from its source to the army posts in the Dakotas and Montana. Although a few floating "luxury palaces" were active, for the most part the boats that traveled the long Missouri weren't in the same class as the pleasure vessels found on the Mississippi.

Life aboard a steamboat on the Missouri was harsh and squalid. The river life that excited the imagination of small boys and grown men also took its toll in human life and suffering.

Clinton learned early to read the water during long, arduous watches. Constant alertness was necessary to avoid the bars, snags, and treacherous rapids, not to mention the half-hidden hulks of less fortunate vessels. The work was backbreaking. Often, the crew would have to go ashore and bury timber in ditches to provide a fastening place for the long cables needed to winch the boat along difficult stretches of the river. Frequently, they would float pieces of scrap lumber, with candles attached and lit, to mark the dangerous channels. Boiler explosions and fires were commonplace, and Missouri steamers sank by the hundreds. Between 1819 and 1900, 300 river boats were destroyed by river hazards on the Missouri; wrecks became accepted as a part of daily life.

When not at the fate of the temperamental vessels, the crews had to contend with hostile Indians firing on them (often requiring pilot's cabins being sheathed in iron). Further, they found it necessary to moor in midstream to avoid being boarded by armed marauders and bandits. It is no wonder these men developed a sense of fatalism and a callous outlook on humanity.

On board, the conditions for crew and passengers alike were often crowded, substandard, and unsafe. Youngsters were constantly falling overboard; sanitation was poor; disease spread quickly; boredom was rampant, and manners were forgotten. Life on board a steamboat was a microcosm of the rougher aspects of frontier life.

The heavy drinking by crew and passengers alike alleviated some monotony, but led to other abuses. The roustabouts (called roosters) were supervised by steamboat mates who often implemented their orders with clubs, knives, and fists. The general character of the crew was brutal, reckless and uneducated. The towns they stopped at to trade or unload and take on supplies were equally lawless, crude, and peopled by hard-pressed men, and occasionally women, who soon lost their battle with the endless muddy streets and heavy traffic of the river. Young men became quickly desensitized.

Captain Oliver Dotson was a learned man for the times and prized his personal library; nevertheless, young Clinton probably learned little beyond reading and writing in the classroom at DeSota. He gained his primary education, from his sixth to sixteenth year, on the river. For him, two worlds existed. One was the world of violence, roughness, bigotry, crudeness and danger; the other the lonely and peaceful beauty of nature. Clinton appreciated the aesthetic side of life, even as a young man, and studied the many birds of the river throughout the seasons.

In 1876, Oliver abandoned the river hauling business. Taking his four oldest sons, he left Nebraska for Cheyenne, Wyoming. Gold was discovered in the Black Hills District of South Dakota in that year, and Oliver considered the area ripe for business. Although the lure of prospecting for gold held him as tightly as ever, he made the practical decision to establish a freighting business between Custer, South Dakota and Cheyenne, Wyoming. If transportation was losing its profitability on water, he reasoned, then perhaps overland transportation would pay off handsomely. After completing necessary business details in Cheyenne, Oliver and his sons took a stage coach to Custer City.

Sixteen year old Clinton was thrilled to be on a stage coach and delighted when, shortly before reaching Custer City, Sioux Indians attacked the coach. Oliver Dotson was an expert marksman, so much so he was barred from entering various amateur competitions. He, along with other well-armed passengers, repelled the attack.

With this adventure under his belt, Clinton and his brothers traveled to Deadwood, South Dakota where they met with the other members of the family. Deadwood was just opening its eyes and there were no houses available, so Oliver and his sons built the family their first house. The house had the distinction of being the second frame house built in Deadwood and it delighted Sarah and her children. It was a palace to young Clinton. The house boasted four large rooms, a wide, covered porch, *ingrain* carpets, sturdy furniture and the family's first luxury–a rocking chair. Clinton worked on the construction of the house, and developed skills which eventually led to him mastering stone masonry.

The next few years of Clinton's life were doubtless the most carefree he experienced. Oliver and his sons capitalized on the freighting business that brought in quick money. Freight lines were essential to the rapidly developing mining communities deep in the beautiful, wooded hills. No railroads penetrated the area and freight rates between Cheyenne and Custer City (twenty-five cents per pound) reflected the scarcity of transportation. Oliver freighted on almost every line into the Black Hills, and supposedly brought the first load of dance hall girls into Deadwood, South Dakota. At first, he used Missouri mule teams, but when the competition became keener, Oliver shrewdly switched to oxen since the beasts were less expensive to feed and house.

As the area was opened and developed, freight lines became more numerous and rates dropped. Oliver gave up the business and put his energy into operating a corral and livery in Deadwood. He accommodated the freighting outfits that were still operating, and found himself profiting from his old competitors. Simultaneously, he took up a claim on 160 acres of land on Spring Creek, north of Spearfish, South Dakota and ran cattle. Frequent Indian raids depleted his herds and he gave up and sold the land a few years later.

Clinton, twenty years old and at loose ends, worked as a stonemason when work was available, but eventually took a job as a cowhand on a ranch outside Cheyenne, Wyoming. Here he met his future wife, Mary Blake, a young woman who worked at a downtown Cheyenne hotel.

Mary Blake, a dark-eyed, dark-haired German woman of sturdy build, was born in Dundee, Illinois in 1862. She was a first generation American and didn't learn to speak English until she was in her teens. She was intelligent, capable, and kind. When she was eighteen years old, she journeyed to Cheyenne, Wyoming alone, leaving her family and friends in North Platte, Nebraska where they had settled. She traveled in the winter of 1880; the trip was long, cold, and uncomfortable. Mary was initiated into the rough way of the frontier almost immediately. A man, traveling on the stage coach, became ill and died en route. His body was placed on top of the stage and securely fastened to the luggage until they could dispose of it properly in Cheyenne. Mary observed with shock the nonchalant manner of the driver as he propped the frozen body up against the coach while he handed down the luggage.

She cooked and waited on tables at a hotel in the brawling cow town for nearly four years. Clinton worked on a ranch out of town, and came into the hotel to enjoy the hearty fare: beefsteak, mutton, biscuits and–inevitably–pie. As he lingered, drinking strong, bitter coffee, he and Mary became acquainted.

Mary felt a strong attraction to Clinton. He'd become a handsome young man, careful of his dress and proud of his smoothly combed black hair. A photograph taken of him at the George W. Scott studio in Deadwood, South Dakota, at approximately this time, shows a tall young man of medium build with a strong, columnar neck tapering into broad shoulders.

The face that looks calmly out of the photographic rendering is rectangular with a strong jaw, high cheekbones, a straight substantial nose, and a neatly trimmed mustache extending slightly downward at the sides of his wide mouth. His ears hug the sides of his head and his right eyebrow arches at its edge, giving him an expression of skepticism.

By far, Clinton's most arresting feature were his eyes: gray, light, direct. Not seen in the picture are his souvenirs from the Missouri River days: a heart, anchor, cross and two spears tattooed over his left nipple.

The relationship flourished and on April 6, 1884, he and Mary were married in Deadwood, Laurence County, Dakota Territory. She was twenty-one years, nine months old; Clinton was just six months short of his twenty-fourth birthday.

Neither Clinton nor Mary had any desire to return to Cheyenne, with its incessant wind and bleak prairie landscape. Instead, they moved to Aladdin, Wyoming, a few miles from the South Dakota border, where they homesteaded and produced their first child, a son, on June 10, 1885, fourteen months after their marriage. The next year Clinton moved Mary's family, her German born parents, two sisters, and three young brothers, to

Aladdin as well. Clinton made the best of it until his brothers-in-law were mature enough to assume responsibility. He then sold out and moved to Deadwood, South Dakota.

There, Clinton worked as a stonemason for the Deadwood Smelting Company, for whom he constructed office buildings. Too soon, however, the work tapered off. His mother Sarah wrote to her brother, Eli, in March 1891.

> I *haven't seen Clinton since last June. He was well the last I heard from him. He only lives sixteen miles from here but I don't get to see him very often. He has a very large family and (they are) very poor. He works by day's wages for a living. We hardly ever see him anymore.*

The family was large; by 1892, he'd fathered four sons and a daughter. When a smallpox epidemic swept the area, he and Mary ran a pest house to care for the victims. Mary managed to care for her family, provide solace and aid to the stricken people of the community, and feed the Indians who, on occasion, either begged or threatened at her kitchen door.

By 1895, Clinton's family had grown to include another son and Mary was pregnant with twins; the family required more money. Gold fever, rampant in the area, manifested itself and Clinton, like his father Oliver, succumbed. He feverishly worked to stake out several claims in Deadwood Gulch, The claims were highly promising and the still-young man dreamed of providing handsomely for his family.

His babies betrayed him: first one, than another, contacted measles until the entire family, Clinton included, had to spend a long, and rigidly enforced, period of quarantine. When Clinton emerged, every one of his claims had been jumped, and he lost his chance at fortune.

The twins, Mary's seventh and eighth offspring, were born on June 5, 1896. Mary's body, depleted by now, couldn't produce enough milk for both and the boy nursed at the breast of a wet nurse, a healthy and robust black woman.

The year 1898 marked a downturn for the family. In June, Mary, worn out from childbearing and suffering from a condition called *milk leg* (a painful swelling of the legs due to thrombophlebitis in the femoral vein, occurring during lactation after childbirth–in her case after the birth of the twins) brought her last child into the world, a girl, weighing only four pounds.

To compound the family's problems, the smelting company shut its doors and left Clinton without even day-labor wages. Clinton moved his family to Crook City (just out of Whitewood, near Sturgis) where he homesteaded forty acres and built a house With their income practically nonexistent, Mary turned to raising potatoes and picking wild berries from the hillside in back of the house. Both were a cash crop, and she regularly drove their old wagon into town and sold from door to door.

Work at the mining company had been desultory for several years before it closed, and Clinton had periodically left his home in search of a job (or a new mining claim), traveling throughout the adjoining states on his horse, camping wherever he stopped for the night. He tried to get back to see his family every month or so and, occasionally, sent them a few dollars.

His father, Oliver, spent the majority of his time in American Gulch, Montana, where he'd built a small cabin and furnished it as a comfortable bachelor's headquarters, replete with his books and several rifles. Oliver spent his days hunting, prospecting, reading, or traveling into Helena to catch up on the latest political news. He was a familiar and respected figure in Helena, striding down the street with his long, white beard spread across his jacket front.

Clinton's mother, Sarah, preferred to stay in Spearfish where Oliver had built her a comfortable home near her children and grandchildren. Cancer took her life in April 1898.

Chapter 6
The Hearing
August 28, 1899

For the week and a half after Benson's interrogation, the law officers made sporadic attempts to elicit more information from Persinger and Dotson, but gained little. *The Anaconda Standard* reported on August 17, 1899, that John Chadwick had gained entrance and demanded "Let me look at the old scoundrel." He apparently relished seeing Clinton behind bars. On August 18, the paper reported that Clinton Dotson had pleaded *not guilty* and a hearing had been set for August 28, 1899, at 2:00 p.m.

The day following the *not guilty* plea, the newspaper revealed the filing of Cullinane's will. He'd left $12,000 to relatives in New England–some of whom had never met the old man.

Clinton spent a fretful ten days. He was sure that by now Mary had learned where he was. He wasn't allowed to write to her yet, and wouldn't know what to tell her when he did write.

His nephew, Charles Benson, put in an even worse ten days. Knowing Benson was the weakest link, the sheriff's officers and County Attorney had kept pressure on him. They exploited his fear of authority, suspecting he'd fled the navy for that very reason. He was unequipped to deal with orders, and the invincible, determined men who issued them. On Friday, August 25, his nerve gave way and he made a damning confession to County Attorney Duffy.

The hearing on Monday morning, August 28, was brief and over before the coolness of morning turned sweltering. Although Dotson and Persinger had pleaded not guilty, Benson's confession–only a portion of the evidence the State had by now secured–was sufficient to charge all three men with first degree murder in the death of Eugene Cullinane. All three were held without bail. A trial was scheduled for the criminal session of district court, starting September 6, 1899.

Clinton's father, Captain Oliver Dotson, was present at the hearing but seemed to pay little attention. The old man, his face stern behind his long, white beard, sat impassively as the defense outlined the evidence against the trio. Mr. Murray, the original owner of the gold watch, positively identified it as one purchased by Cullinane. A vest, worn by Benson at the time of arrest, but purported to be Dotson's, was produced. In the pocket of the garment was a memorandum book in which diary-like notations, supposedly in Dotson's hand, further condemned Clinton.

Oliver showed no interest in the evidence, not even looking up when his son denied all knowledge of the book. The old man, his hands clasped on his cane, heard his son charged with murder and ordered to trial. The next day, after refusing to pay for an attorney for his son, he went back to his cabin.

Chapter 7
The Trial
October 5, 1899

The trial began on October 5, 1899, five days before Clinton's thirty-ninth birthday. The strong jailhouse coffee brought to him in his cell that morning left a bitter taste in his mouth, and made him long for his home. He'd planned to spend his birthday with his family, enjoying a slice of the *kuchen* Mary baked for special occasions.

It took nearly a month beyond the original September 6 trial date for the State to locate and subpoena witnesses. In all, they secured forty-two people to testify. Some were reluctant when they found out the state wouldn't pay for their mileage, but came nevertheless to help the prosecution condemn Clinton Dotson.

They were an oddly assorted group, as evidenced from a document signed by Sheriff Conley and Deputy Sheriff Daly, dated October 3, 1899. In the document, they state that they served subpoenas to the following:

John Chadwick's hired man, near Washington Gulch, whose name is Wm. Annet.
Big Jeff, Policeman, Helena, Montana whose name is Jeff O'Connell.
Man who tends bar nearly opposite the Salvation Army Barracks in Helena, Montana, and whose wife was a delegate to the A.O.U. W. Grand Lodge in Butte, whose name is C. H. Colbath.
John Chadwick and Gabriel Hilderbrand, Washington Gulch.
Mrs. Upgard, Helena, Montana (called "Crazy Emma").
H. H. Ashley (not John Ashley) man with bill of sale from Dotson and Benson.
Ed Cachelin, Washington Gulch.
George F. Ingram, Helena, Montana.

Harry Winters, who was supposed to work at Capitol Saloon, Helena, but who works at Office Saloon, Helena.
Frank Conley, Deer Lodge, Montana.
John Conley and D. H. Morgan, Anaconda.
John Simington, State Prison, Deer Lodge, Montana.

The case was called in the District Court in Anaconda at 9:30 a.m. Thursday morning. County Attorney J. H. Duffy, Deputy John T. Casey, and Deputy J. J. Walsh conducted the prosecution.

After Oliver Dotson had stated he wouldn't pay for an attorney for his son, the State had appointed attorneys W.H. Trippet and J. M. Self as counsel for the defense. While the two lawyers were preparing a case, and securing twenty-four witnesses for the defense, Clinton's father, Oliver, made conflicting statements to the press. Some of these statements were highly damaging to Clinton, but of great interest to the reading public.

On September 10, 1899, *The Anaconda Standard* quoted the old man as saying that his son was guilty and should hang, and confirmed that the old man refused to defend his son. The reporter said that a neighbor came forth to support Oliver:

The Dotson family is well known to me. For years we lived neighbors in the Black Hills. Captain Oliver Dotson is one of the squarest men that ever lived and gives no countenance to the crime even if committed by relatives. He (Dotson) said, "Son of mine or not, he should hang."

Public opinion was running strongly against the three accused men and Oliver was having a hard time holding his head up in front of his friends and neighbors. The crime had aroused and angered everyone in American and Washington Gulches, as well as the citizens of Helena and the surrounding small towns. A respected and well-liked old man had been brutally murdered for a few dollars and a gold watch. The pressure on Oliver was great, and both his pride and his sense of self-preservation

43

compelled him to stand with the rest of the community and against his son.

Once the trial had started, however, paternal concern asserted itself and Oliver showed signs of changing his position. Oliver was called upon by both the defense and the prosecution at the trial and testified for both. On October 12, he told a writer for *The Anaconda Standard* he was "upset" that it was reported he would not help his son. He said that, "Regardless of Clinton's innocence or guilt, he would make every effort and sacrifice to save him." The problem was he possessed scant means and his property wasn't convertible into cash. This was probably true, since he'd been unable to put up his own bail, and had to accept the help of his son-in-law, Edward Cachelin, when the two of them had been arrested earlier.

The tall, white-haired old man with the sad face watched helplessly as the trial progressed.

The Deer Lodge City newspaper, *The Silver State* reported on October 11, 1899,

Quite a time was had in securing a jury, as most everyone had read of the case and formed or expressed an opinion as to the guilt or innocence of the accused. The regular panel was soon exhausted, when a special venire (venire facias: a writ or order) of 100 names was issued, and not until another call for 50 or more was made was a jury in the case secured on Saturday afternoon (October 7). The principal witnesses not being present, the jury was instructed by Judge Napton and court adjourned until Monday morning. The jury which was closely guarded by two bailiffs, (Deputies Tom Mullen and J. J. Walsh) while not on duty, is composed of the following:

    Andrew Peterson, of Warm Springs, farmer
    Luke Talbot, of Stuart, farmer
    William Dengler, Sr., of Anaconda, miner
    Frank Christoffersen, of Deer Lodge, farmer
    Albert R. Kleist, of Anaconda, drayman

Frederick Zimmerman, of Anaconda, butcher
John Sanders, of Cable, farmer
A. E. Schwend, of Anaconda
J.N. Emmons of Carroll, Farmer
Henry Williams, Mechanical Engineer, Anaconda
James McGrady, of Anaconda, laborer
Lafayette Scott, of Deer Lodge, Laborer

The jury contained a preponderance of farmers, perhaps because these men had been more occupied with tilling the soil, harvesting, and preparing for the coming cruel Montana winter than with reading the lurid newspaper accounts of the crime or listening to the inflamed street-corner talk of lynching and swift justice. Few, if any of them, would realize that until the last year or so, Clinton had led a life not greatly different from theirs–one of toil, hard work, worry, family.

While the jury spent Sunday under guard, the lawyers for the defense worked feverishly to coordinate their case and prepare their witness roster. Clinton languished in his cell, alternately charged with nervous energy, then felled with despair and apathy. He felt absolutely powerless, more so once he knew that his nephew had made a damning statement condemning him.

Chapter 8
Opening Day
October 9, 1899

On Monday morning, the trial began in earnest. All the witnesses, forty-two for the State and twenty-four for the defense, had been sworn in. The courtroom was packed with a crowd, angry and righteous, anticipating the appearance of the "scoundrel" Dotson.

It was a crisp October day. A brisk wind stirred the dry autumn leaves, and whipped color into the already weather-burned faces of the jurors as they hurried into the courtroom. Few of the men were happy with the interruption of their labor; they hoped to get their civic duty over quickly.

When Clinton Dotson was escorted into the room, the members of the jury examined him closely. From their seats, they viewed Clinton in profile, a thin man with graying hair and a grave expression on his smoothly shaven face. He wore a dark jacket and trousers; a light-colored shirt was buttoned closely around his neck. His appearance hardly fit the rough, lawless, *bully* image given him by the press.

He was seated facing the window, and seemed to be gazing at a bank of heavy clouds building up over the mountains, oblivious to the commotion his entrance had stirred in the spectators.

Throughout the long morning, while County Attorney Duffy opened the case and read the complaint, Clinton sat woodenly. The only movement discernible was that of his never-still jaws: he was chewing tobacco as a substitute for his pipe.

When Duffy began speaking, a hush fell over the courtroom and he commanded everyone's undivided attention as they eagerly listened to the details of the crime. He methodically

46

outlined for the jury the events surrounding the discovery of Eugene Cullinane's body: the evidence found at the scene; the alleged proposition Clinton Dotson, the defendant, made to a neighbor of Cullinane's concerning killing and robbing the old man; the chase for the murderers; the arrest of Dotson, Persinger, and Benson; the incriminating evidence found in the wagon; the description of the wagon, and the route that the men were known to have taken–eastward from the scene of the murder.

The first witness called was Dr. Glass, a local physician who had the duty of conducting an examination of the body. County Attorney Duffy quickly covered the doctor's identification and qualifications, establishing that the man had practiced medicine for thirty years, the last seventeen of which were in Deer Lodge County. Additionally, he'd been acquainted with Eugene Cullinane and verified he'd seen the body at the morgue, a facility belonging to Mr. Bien, the undertaker. Duffy got down to business quickly:

Q. What wounds or bruises did you discover about or on the body?

A. Well, there was three wounds.

Q. Give me the point of entrance of the cut or wounds as near as you can and describe the course of the bullet or bullets and describe through what tissues, arteries and vessels the bullet traveled in its course.

A. The first wound was on the upper part of the right arm, penetrating the flesh.

Q. Was it a shattered wound?

A. I could not tell whether or not it was a shattered wound and how it happened to get there, as I did not see the body in its original state after death.

Q. That wound that you saw upon the arm, it was not what you would call necessarily fatal was it?

A. No sir, not necessarily fatal.

Q. Describe the next wound.

A. The next wound was external, the bullet entering a point between the ear and the nose half ways between the lower part of the upper maxilla bone, part of the jaw bone.

Q. On what side of the nose?

A. On the left.

Q. Where was the exit of the bullet?

A. The exit was at the back, about an inch and a half from the spine below the occipital bone, back of the right ear.

Q. Was the wound necessarily fatal?

A. It was necessarily fatal. It was fatal, yes sir.

Duffy let the effect of the words sink in for a moment, then pressed the point further.

Q. Sufficient to cause death?

A. Probably not instantly, but it would have in a question of time.

Q. I will ask you to state if you, in conjunction with any other physician, made an autopsy of the body of Eugene Cullinane. If you did, state in detail the result of the autopsy.

A. Dr. Ownings was there.

Q. State the result of the examination made.

A. The second bullet entered the back about three inches from the spine and passed below the floating ribs and penetrated the kidney, cut the renal artery, and lodged in the forepart of the abdomen. The bullet penetrated through the body and a dark black spot could be seen from the outside. The bullet penetrated through the body and lodged in the fore part of the abdomen.

Q. Then the bullet laid between two layers before going out of the body?

A. Yes sir.

Q. So that wound with the other two, in your judgment, were of a character sufficient to produce death.

A. Instant death.

Q. Instantaneous death?

A. Yes sir.

Duffy then elicited from the venerable, if somewhat disheveled, doctor that the wound on the face was probably the first one Eugene received, followed by the wound on the back. Duffy next made a point that, in itself, could easily send a man to the gallows in turn-of-the-century Montana. He established that Eugene Cullinane had been shot in the back. Dr. Glass stood and demonstrated how Cullinane was probably standing when both bullets entered his body.

Deputy Walsh was the next to question Glass and he, too, irrevocably established that Eugene had first received a face wound, then was shot in the back. The doctor pointed out that had he been shot in the back first, he would have fallen forward and couldn't have been shot in the face, as all evidence showed. Walsh verified the credibility of the examination while the audience in the courtroom leaned forward to hear the grisly details.

Q. What was the condition of the body at the time you held the autopsy?

A. It was in pretty good condition.

Q. About how long had this man been dead at the time you made the examination?

A. I don't know whether the undertaker used any embalming fluid or not, to keep the body from decay, it seems to me that he must have been dead three or four days.

Q. In reference to the wound on the arm, did you examine it closely to see what kind of wound it was?

A. I could not tell.

Q. What is the reason you could not tell?

A. The man had on a great many clothes, and it looked as though the clothes had been torn. It was a skin wound and I could not tell whether it was made by a bullet or not.

Duffy returned to question the doctor, who was having difficulty remembering just what day it was he'd examined the body. The physician thought it might have been the twentieth of the month, until Duffy pointed out that it was "two weeks ago Sunday that you made the autopsy." Duffy recalled he'd attended a baseball game a week ago, on a Sunday, and that it was the week before the game that the autopsy had taken place. Dr. Glass agreed it probably was.

There was little the defense could do other than make an issue of the Doctor's faulty memory. They chose not to, realizing more harm than good might come of it.

The Anaconda Standard reported that, throughout the first day of the trial, Clinton, a "cold, gray man" failed to be moved by the evidence building up against him. One observer commented, "My, what a poker player that man would make."

Clinton glanced up only briefly when Deputy Sheriff John Robinson took the stand, then gazed out at the mountains again, concentrating on the foreboding clouds that were gradually blurring the outline of the taller hills.

Sheriff Robinson didn't look like a daring law officer any more than Clinton looked like a roughneck outlaw. In another setting, the two men could have easily passed for businessmen discussing the finer points of commerce.

Robinson was of average size, tastefully but simply dressed, and of unprepossessing demeanor. His darkish hair topped a high, finely molded forehead. He had a long, symmetrically shaped nose and a neatly trimmed mustache that sloped downward on each side. His most arresting features were his Edgar Allan Poe eyes, dark and melancholy. His appearance was misleading: John Robinson was crafty, ambitious, dedicated to his career, and as hard as nails.

County Attorney Duffy began the questioning, first establishing that Robinson was the Deputy Sheriff in Deer Lodge County.

Q. In your official capacity had you occasion to make the arrest of these three men?
A. I did.
Q. Where did you find them?

A. I made the arrest on a wagon road east of a place called Central Park, in Gallatin County.

Q. State whether or not the three of them had been traveling together?

A. I saw them together before they were arrested.

Q. At the time of the arrest were they together or separate?

A. I saw them together, these two men, Dotson and Benson, were together.

Q. Where was Persinger?

A. Well, they said he was at a store about a mile from there.

Q. What were they traveling in?

A. Two horses and a wagon.

Q. Will you describe the horses, size, color and peculiar marks of identification, what the wagon was covered with?

A. It was a spring wagon, end and side springs, the spokes were wrapped with wire, and it had a big white canvas cover with a big, black patch in it right on top of the cover.

Q. The bows then were covered with a white canvas cover?

A. Yes, with the exception of a big, black patch on the top of it.

Q. Describe the horses.

A. There were two bay horses, one of them was branded with "A" on the left hip and "J" on the right jaw, that was the lightest colored bay. I did not find brands on the darker colored one.

After describing the horses, Robinson said that the wheels of the wagon didn't leave a true track; the right-hand wheel had a bent axle and it wobbled, making an irregular track. This was important testimony, and Duffy gave it his full attention.

Q. Did the wayward wheel make a peculiar track?

A. The track that was made by the hind wheel would run outside of the track made by the front wheel on that side.

Duffy then got to the next piece of evidence. The jury shifted in their seats, but still listened attentively.

Q. State whether or not you made a search of the wagon in which they were and if so, what you found in that wagon.

A. I made a pretty thorough search, I found lots of things.

Q. Describe them.

A. Pots, kettles, knives, forks, spoons, etc.

Q. I will ask you if you found a watch there.

A. I did.

The spectators let out a collective sigh. Now, the defense was getting down to business. Many had been waiting for this point in the trial–at least a third of them had seen the watch proudly displayed by the old miner and knew it was the most damning piece of physical evidence. The defense had examined the State's exhibits on September 17, but didn't have enough information to refute either Cullinane's ownership of the timepiece or Clinton's possession of it. Clinton grimly chewed his tobacco, his jaws working rhythmically.

Q. Describe to the court where you found that watch.

A. The watch was found by the sheriff of Gallatin County. I threw the mattress on the ground and told him to cut it open and look around in there. He says, 'Look here, I found something.' I went over to where he was; it was near one end of the mattress that he found the watch.

Q. Do you know how the watch was put in the mattress?

A. No sir.

Q. Was there a hole in the mattress where the watch was found?

A. There was no hole in that part of the mattress. There was one hole in the mattress but not where the watch was found. I did not see it; it must have been sewn up.

Robinson stated that he'd turned the watch over to the Sheriff and it had been in his possession since. Duffy asked him to examine the watch and verify it was the same one found in the defendant's possession. Robinson stated, "This is the same watch unless there is another one made exactly like it. The numbers and marks and everything correspond exactly with the numbers I took from it at the time."

After further verification, the watch was introduced into evidence and marked as Exhibit "A." The Deputy Sheriff also stated that he'd found considerable clothing in the decrepit wagon, but that he'd not paid particular attention to any of it. He put it all in two valises along with a telescope found in the men's possession. The two valises, plus two overcoats too bulky to fit inside, were placed in a vault in the sheriff's office in Bozeman. From there, Robinson had them shipped to Anaconda, picked them up at the depot, and took them to the sheriff's office. He'd not been present when they were opened.

Duffy next turned to the discovery of Eugene Cullinane's hastily interred body.

Q. You are the gentleman who found the body of Eugene Cullinane?
A. I found the body.
Q. Describe where you found the body, the position it was in and what, if any, examination you made around the immediate vicinity in reference to tracks, what tracks you found, and what size shoe they were made with.

Robinson took a deep breath, preparing to answer the fusillade of questions. Duffy tended to ask a long string of questions in rapid sequence, more to impress the jury with the weight of the evidence than to elicit an answer. He then would go back and ask his questions point for point. The effect of these barrages was positive–the jury straightened up, leaned forward like saplings in a high wind, and paid attention.

A. I found the body about a half a mile in an easterly direction from what they said was his cabin. I don't know whether or not it was his cabin. I was about 20 feet below the water ditch, it was in a ravine about, well, from 10 to 20 feet on the left hand side of the road going up the gulch. I didn't measure it, it was probably 10 feet. It might have been 20 feet but I don't think it was over 20 feet. It was in a little place that looked like the water had washed over it, it was laid in there covered up.

Q. With what?

A. Brush, dirt and leaves.

Q. What was the condition of the clothing on the corpse at the time you found it?

A. The clothes was ripped off the body like they had been cut or torn.

Q. Where were they placed in reference to the face and head?

A. There was leaves and brush and dirt over the face.

Q. About how deep was he buried?

A. I don't think there was over three or four inches of dirt and stuff over the body.

Q. After you found the body what was done next?

A. I uncovered the face and asked the parties that were there with me if that was the man we were looking for. They said it was.

Q. Do you know who took charge of it?

A. A man by the name of Kessinger, and Mulholland.

Duffy asked several routine questions to establish the county in which the body had been found. He then asked about the wagon tracks and shoe prints.

Robinson replied, "I made an examination of the country around there in a hurried way. I found two tracks, one made with a pointed toe shoe, and one made with a large flat shoe. The shoe making the pointed print was about a number 7. A smaller shoe than I wear."

He thrust his right foot forward as though to prove his point. The jury's eyes swung from his foot to Clinton's. Dotson shifted in his chair but didn't move either foot. Duffy pressed on.

Q. What was the size of the shoe that made the flat track?

A. Eight at least.

Q. That was the largest track?

A. Yes sir.

Q. Did you examine the tracks to see whether there was a running down on either side of the heel?
A. I did not.
Q. How far were these tracks distant?
A. The only place I saw them was a little place where the water run over forming a sandbar there, that's the only place I seen them.

Duffy sat, satisfied, and Deputy Walsh took over the examination of Robinson. Though not as concise as the prosecutor would have liked for him to be, Robinson had a strong, clear voice and spoke sincerely and directly to the jury. Mr. Walsh led the Deputy Sheriff slowly through the events of the capture. Robinson said that neither Benson nor Dotson acknowledged they had any idea why they were arrested. Persinger, arrested by another officer, was brought to the campsite within a half hour and was present when the search for the watch was conducted. All three men, guarded by the deputies, had been approximately 20 feet from the mattress as the law officers ripped it open. Robinson reiterated that nothing was said by the prisoners when the watch was discovered.

The reporters in the courtroom shook their heads sadly; unless the defense could refute any of the prosecution's statements, the trial was going to be shorter and less dramatic than they had hoped.

Chapter 9
Clinton's Birthday
October 10, 1899

The trustee greeted Clinton, on the morning of his thirty-ninth birthday, with a cup of scalding coffee and a substantial breakfast; the weather greeted him with a brisk wind and bright blue skies; the prosecution greeted him with Mr. John Mulholland, Eugene Cullinane's cabin mate and grieving friend.

County Attorney Duffy, refreshed and eager, wasted no time in establishing that Mulholland and Cullinane had been roommates off and on for about four years. John had last seen the old prospector alive on August 2, 1899. He stated he'd identified the body and that Eugene did indeed have a gold watch, acquired in a Helena pawn shop from Tom Murray.

Mr. Murray was next to take the stand. Duffy was now working up a good head of steam, and the questions came fast and sure. Mr. Murray quickly confirmed that he worked in a pawnbroker's shop and had sold the watch to Cullinane in August 1896. He pulled out his memorandum book and compared the watch number recorded there with the watch proffered by the prosecution as evidence. "Yes," he said, "it was the same watch, and watch numbers were never duplicated."

Deputy Walsh then took over while the satisfied County Attorney sat, leaned back in his chair, and leveled an even stare at Clinton. The defendant sat as quietly as the day before; only his jaw worked, worrying the tobacco evenly, occasionally shifting it from one side to the other. A pallor lay about his face, and his gray eyes and graying hair did nothing to lift the somberness of his person. The "cold, gray man" of the reporter's

56

pen was just that; he elicited no sympathy from the jurors, any of whom could have been his victim.

From the women in the courtroom, however, he drew kinder reactions. Some responded maternally, evaluating his thin physique and sad, withdrawn expression. They knew a few hearty meals, as only they could prepare them, would fill out his frame in no time at all. For the younger, or more bored women in the hard frontier mining town, Clinton had a certain air of mystery about him. He was a handsome man, even as worn and solemn as he appeared, and his reserve and indifference allowed them to create whatever personality or past escapades they chose for him. Additionally, outlaws weren't without their charm, particularly as described by the press.

Deputy Walsh quickly finished questioning Tom Murray, but gained no additional information other than the fact that every time Murray had met with Cullinane, he'd seen the watch in Cullinane's possession. He'd not, however, seen the watch since last March or April, he wasn't sure which. Murray couldn't say if Eugene Cullinane had the watch in his possession at the time of his death.

The next witness called by the State was Mr. Hammerslough, a jeweler who appeared as respectable, weighty, and ponderous as his name.

Q. What is your business?
A. Jeweler.
Q. How long have you been engaged in the jewelry business?
A. Ten years.
Q. Are you acquainted with the custom of manufacturers, in referencing to placing numbers upon the works of watches?
A. I am.
Q. Do different manufacturers have the same numbers?
A. Makers do.
Q. How do the numbers run?
A. The numbers run from one upwards.
Q. Do the numbers on the case and the numbers of the works of the same watch correspond?

A. No sir.
Q. Look at this watch and see where it was manufactured. Look at the case and the works.
A. The case was manufactured by the American Watch Company.
Q. Waltham movement?
A. Yes sir.
Q. It is very easy to tell the real Waltham movement?
A. Yes sir, there is no movement made like the Waltham.
Q. What is the number on this watch?
A. 2548000.

The prosecution had now established a strong case against the defendants based on identification of the wagon, matching wagon tracks and shoe prints, and, more damning, the gold watch belonging to Cullinane but found hidden in the mattress in the old spring wagon. Now, one more piece of evidence was produced through the testimony of Dave Morgan, an undersheriff of Deer Lodge County. Duffy asked Morgan:

Q. Did you have occasion in your official duties to examine a grip sack or valise referred to by Mr. Robinson?
A. Yes sir.
Q. Was there a vest in that valise?
A. Yes.
Q. I will ask you to describe what you found in that vest in the way of books.
A. There was a memorandum book in one of the pockets.
Q. You found in the vest a little memorandum book?
A. Yes sir.
Q. I will ask you if that vest was afterwards taken to Deer Lodge and shown to the defendant, Dotson?
A. Yes sir.
Q. Whose vest did he say it was?
A. He said it was his.
Q. You say it was in the vest that you found this memorandum book?

A. Yes sir.

Q. Were you present at the time Benson made any statement on the 25th of this month, in reference to this prosecution that we are now hearing?

A. Yes sir.

Q. It was made freely and voluntarily?

A. Yes sir.

Q. State what was said.

A. He said when he made the statements he knew that any statements he made would be used against him on his trial.

Duffy held up the vest.

Q. Mr. Morgan, is that the identical vest?

A. Yes sir.

Walsh stepped in and said, "I will now introduce this vest with its contents, this book. It is a confession by Dotson stating where he was at the time of this killing."

Clinton's attorney was instantly on his feet. "We object to the introduction of the book in evidence."

He leaned over and spoke quickly and quietly to the defendant. The use of the word "confession" by Deputy J. J. Walsh had its calculated effect on the jury, although the book was little more than a record of travel and hardly constituted a confession. The jurors listened with even more attention to the rest of Mr. Morgan's testimony. Clinton, too, was listening with avid interest now.

The subject was the confession, called "sensational" by the press, which his nephew and traveling companion, Charles Benson, had allegedly made on August 25, 1899. A flicker of disgust and concern crossed Clinton's face as Deputy Morgan discussed Benson's statement.

Morgan stated that the young man had made the confession in the sheriff's office at the court house—that Benson "spoke up and said he wanted to tell the truth" and that he'd been

59

"interviewed two or three times" by the officers before making his statement.

Morgan emphasized that Benson had been fully apprised of his rights and that no inducements had been made–nor threats extended–to get him to freely speak of the crime. Morgan stated that at the time Benson had made his first statement (on August 16) "probably all the sheriff's officers were there, there was probably twelve or fifteen persons in the room at that time."

Morgan stepped down and the prosecution moved smoothly into the grand finale–the details of Benson's confession and the introduction of the confession as evidence.

County Attorney, Duffy, was sworn in and questioned by his colleague, Walsh. Duffy was even more formidable on the stand than off. He was an articulate and dignified presence who, patiently and carefully, explained the procedure to the jury– without seeming to talk down to the lesser learned men who, in the course of their ordinary lives, had little contact with courts and legal language. He testified, clearly and without pause:

I will state that this written document here was signed by Charles Oliver Benson in my presence after it had been read over to him and after he was told he could make any corrections that he desired to make. He did suggest one correction–which correction was promptly made. This statement was made freely and voluntarily by him after he had been informed of the charge against him, being told that this was a murder case, and that his statement, if he made any, would be used against him as well as against Dotson and Persinger. That he was under no obligation to make any statements to me or anybody else, that he had a right to remain silent and refuse to utter a word to anybody, that my purpose was to get the truth. That is what my business as County Attorney required me to do, that there was to be no promises made to him of any kind or character and if he was to make a statement at all, it was to be of his own free will and made freely and voluntarily. It was first taken down by a stenographer, and after a transcript was made it was read over to him and signed by him. I will say further that I took this confession to the penitentiary where Persinger and Dotson were confined. I read it over to each of them in the presence of Jack Conley. One of the guards was also present. I informed them fully as to their rights and asked them what they had to say about it. They said nothing. Dotson was asked the direct question by Jack Conley. He said he had nothing to say. Persinger made use of the remark 'I expected it, I thought that they would try to swear it on me.' That was substantially the statement made by Persinger in the office of the State Penitentiary at Deer Lodge.

Duffy was next asked how many conversations he had with Benson and replied, "Three." He indicated the first was when the trio was arrested; the second was when a witness from Elliston, Montana identified Benson as one of the party he had seen traveling in the old wagon; the third time was to secure the confession. Duffy said,

I returned to Anaconda Thursday night about 11 o'clock and the next morning about noon on Friday, that would be last Friday, I went down to the jail. Mr. Benson was in the jail in a cell at the extreme left on the south side of the corridor. He was brought out from there into this jury room and I told him I was there for the purpose of listening to any statement he might make. I told him the first statement he made was not true; remember anything you say will be used against you. I am not making any promises to you, there will be no threats made, or inducements offered. He substantially repeated this confession. I said, 'Mr. Benson, we will have to let this go until this afternoon as there is no reporter present. I will come back this afternoon and bring a stenographer to take down your statements.' He then made the statements that are here in this confession.

Q. At whose solicitation were each of these interviews had?

A. At mine. I wanted to see them and get the truth. I then told them if they wished to be represented by an attorney, to mention the attorney's name and I would send word to that attorney.

Q. At any time did they request an interview?

A. No.

The full confession of Charles Oliver Benson was introduced into evidence and marked as Exhibit "B." In it, the confused, slowwitted and vague young man suddenly became sure, fluent, and chronologically and geographically astute. It is doubtful he could have accomplished this metamorphosis without strong coaching, although it was vigorously denied. Benson used legal terms and words beyond his vocabulary and capability.

The opening paragraph of the confession read as follows:

CONFESSION:

I, Charles Oliver Benson, do this 25th day of August 1899, in the presence of J. H. Duffy, County Attorney of Deer Lodge County, Jack Conley, Dave Morgan, Joe Stephens, and Jack Walsh, of my own free will and without any promises having been made to me, no inducements held out to me, no reward offered me, and without any threats being made to me, do make this my own free and voluntary confession, and I do make this after being informed by J. H. Duffy, County Attorney of Deer Lodge County, that the same will be used against me on my trial, as well as against Clinton Dotson and Ellis Persinger, and after I need not make this statement unless I voluntarily wish to do so and I was told that I would not be rewarded in any way whatever and no promise of any kind, character, or description would be offered or held out to me.

The balance of the written confession presented to the court seemed to be a composite of the question and answer session that incriminated Clinton Dotson, Ellis Persinger, and Benson himself. It read:

Q. Mr. Benson, will you please state what time yourself, Persinger, and Dotson left the town of Helena and by what means you left?

A. We left on the morning of August 5 in the same wagon and drawn by the same horses that the officers afterwards found in our possession on the day of our arrest. We traveled out going from Helena, Montana, in the direction of Washington Gulch, 15 miles on said fifth day of August where we camped for the night. We remained there that night in camp. The next morning, the morning of the sixth, about 7 o'clock that morning we continued our journey, still going in the direction of Washington Gulch and in the direction of the home of Eugene Cullinane, and traveled out on that day about ten miles where we stopped and remained until it got about dark, when the day became about dark we three continued on to travel all that night, the night of the 6th of August, still going in the direction of Eugene Cullinane's home. We continued on our travels the night of the sixth until we stopped a little while before daylight, on the morning of the seventh at Nevada Creek. We stayed there all that day and camped and hid the horses and wagon in the brush, where the rig could not be observed nor seen.

Q. Did you remain in that place all night?

A. We remained there all night of the seventh together, and on the morning of the eighth, and before daylight of that morning, Dotson and Persinger left me in charge of the rig there and went towards the direction of Eugene Cullinane's place. I knew they were going there to rob him, because they had frequently talked about robbing him before we left Helena and after we left Helena. Dotson said that he knew that the old man had money and had considerable money buried in and around his place. Before they left on the morning of the eighth about daylight, each of them took a weapon out of the wagon that we had been traveling in,

63

Dotson taking a .38 caliber rifle which was afterward found in the wagon by the officers when they made the arrest of myself, Dotson, and Persinger. They were gone all that day of the 8th of August 1899. They did not get any money from the old man, so they said. Where the wagon was here, hidden in the brush, was at a point about a mile and a half from Eugene's cabin, I should judge. I did not hear any shots fired. I did not know how many were fired. Dotson upon his return answered. "We will have to get out of here now." I did not ask him the reason why. I supposed the reason.

When Dotson returned towards the evening of the eighth, Persinger was with him at that time, to wit; Dotson had two pair of shoes and I think wore a pair of pointed shoes, and Persinger wore a pair of shoes that were not as pointed as Dotson's. Dotson wore a number 7 or 8 shoe, and Persinger about a 9 shoe, I think. Both of them, Dotson and Persinger, told me they had got no money from the old man. I knew that on the morning of the eighth, they started to the old man's place for the purpose of robbing him of his money. After Dotson and Persinger returned to where the wagon was concealed in the brush on the evening of the eighth, we waited until it got dark and we hitched up the horses and drove them towards Helena. The wagon that we rode in had the bows and slats which were for the purpose of supporting a canvas cover. I first saw Cullinane's watch or the watch that was in the mattress of the wagon when we were arrested, and either Dotson or Persinger, I do not know which, threw it in the bed and told me to swear with them that Persinger bought it from a stranger near our camp at Helena. There was no stranger, or no man at any time while we were in Helena, sold either of us the watch that was afterwards found in the mattress by the officers when they made the arrest. While in jail at Bozeman, Dotson and Persinger (told me to say) they bought the watch that was afterwards found in the mattress aforesaid from a stranger. I agreed to do so. My statement in that respect was false and untrue. I made it because Persinger and Dotson requested me to make it. I now desire to state the truth. After leaving the place where we had the wagon hid, about a mile and a half from Eugene Cullinane's place, we traveled the night.

Q. In what direction?

A. Towards Helena. On our way to Helena, we passed by Blackfoot. While at Nevada Creek, I saw a team which I took to be a butcher's wagon.

Q. When you went through Blackfoot City?

A. No sir.

Q. What time was it?

A. About 12 o'clock at night. We passed through Blackfoot City going towards Helena. At about midnight on the 8th of August. We continued on our way the balance of the night and finally arrived at Helena the night of the 9th of August and remained in Helena the tenth and eleventh.

Q. Where abouts in Helena?

A. We was camped down there by Central Park. We camped while in Helena near a sampling mill and near Central Park. I do not know how long Dotson had known Persinger. Dotson first formed the acquaintance of Persinger while I was not with him. I have frequently heard Dotson and Persinger prior to the 5th of August talk about robbing old man Cullinane of his money and that they intended to get the money and this was the purpose of leaving Helena and going to Washington Gulch. I did not get none of the money nor they did not agree to give me any of the money.

Q. Did they make any statement to you that when, if you were arrested, that you would all tell the same story about this watch.

A. Yes, it was agreed between us that we would all tell the same story–to the effect that Persinger bought the watch from a stranger. As above stated, I make this statement freely and voluntarily, expecting no reward, and no promises have been made to me, but with a purpose to tell the truth and the whole truth, and let my punishment be what it may. I did not consent to go with Dotson or Persinger voluntarily, but was induced by them to go with them for the purpose of robbing Eugene Cullinane. I lied when I said we had nothing to do with robbing Cullinane.

(signed) C. O. Benson
(Witness signature)
J. H. Duffy
Joseph Daly
Jack Walsh

Subscribed and sworn to before me this 25 day of August, 1899.

(Signed) J. H. Duffy
County Attorney of Deer Lodge County

On October 11, 1899, *The Silver State* reported:

Notwithstanding, the prisoner is possessed of unusual nerve and is not moved by the evidence so far, the testimony has been most damaging to him. Unless the attorneys for the defense have something up their sleeve, Dotson is a condemned man. They have not given out their line of defense, but it is believed it will lie in an effort to prove an alibi. There are some six or seven witnesses yet to be examined for the prosecution, after which the defense will introduce its evidence. It is not expected the verdict will be reached before Friday evening. The case of Oliver Benson, nephew of the accused, is set for tomorrow, and today Judge Napton ordered issued a special venire for 100 names, for jurors, which are made returnable at 2 o'clock tomorrow, but this case cannot come up until the one now on is disposed of.

The defense didn't have anything up their sleeve. Clinton, swaying from side to side in the witness chair like a man in a trance, didn't help his case. He simply denied any knowledge of the crime whatsoever.

The jury thought otherwise. On October 12, Thursday afternoon, after only deliberating for two hours, the foreman, Lafayette Scott, a laborer from Deer Lodge, submitted a handwritten document that stated in large, looped letters–and misspelled words–Clinton's fate.

We the jury empanneled to try the above cause find the defendant, Clinton Dotson, guilty of murder in the second degree and fix his punishment at Ninty Nine years in the State Penitentiary.

(signed) Lafayette Scott

Foreman

Chapter 10
The Sentencing
October 13, 1899

At two o'clock on Friday afternoon, Judge Napton formally sentenced Clinton to ninety-nine years at hard labor in the Montana Territorial Prison at Deer Lodge, Montana. The judge pointed out that the charge was reduced to Murder in the Second Degree, since the jury had been unable to agree on the first degree murder charge. Judge Napton asked Clinton if he'd anything to say. Clinton looked around the courtroom, now nearly empty except for his attorneys and the Prosecuting Attorney Duffy. He fixed his eyes on the elaborately carved oak bench and replied: "I don't know as I have."

Attorney James Self stepped forward and tried a last, desperate appeal to the judge.

> Your Honor, if it pleases the court, on behalf of my client, Clinton Dotson, I want to advise you this man has a wife and nine children living in Whitewood, South Dakota. This good woman is totally without funds or means of supporting herself. This man's family is destitute, your honor, totally destitute. Without her husband's support, she can neither feed, shelter, nor keep her family together. We would ask your consideration of this circumstance in the sentencing.

On hearing his attorney put into words what he'd been agonizing over in his own mind, Clinton lost his nerve and broke down. He sat silently shedding tears, making no effort to wipe them away or to stop them.

Judge Napton solemnly confirmed that Clinton must spend the rest of his life in prison. A tremor passed through Clinton's body; his throat choked and for several minutes he was unable to speak. When he found his voice, he murmured, "I would rather they had hanged me than give me life."

Oliver visited his son that afternoon at the jail and tried to console him. Now that the pressure was off, Oliver could totally side with his son. He reassured Clinton that he would begin at once to do all he could for him.

A newspaper article in *The Silver State* on October 18, 1899, wasn't so sympathetic.

Dotson Will Not Hang
Found guilty of Murder in the Second Degree
Benson Pleads Guilty to Manslaughter and is Sentenced for Ten Years
Persinger's Case Put Off Until November 21

Clinton Dotson, in the district court, at Anaconda, on trial for the murder of Eugene Cullinane of American Gulch, was found guilty of murder in the second degree by a jury, last Thursday evening, and sentenced to the pen for 99 years. It is needless to say the verdict was a great disappointment to the public and to the sheriff's officers and county attorney.

The officers took Clinton to the penitentiary on Saturday morning. After being admitted, he sat in his cell, sick at heart. On writing day, he planned to write his first letter to Mary. The only positive aspect of their poverty was that she couldn't afford to travel to the trial – nor could she leave the children for that long; the twins were only three years old, the baby girl only a little over a year. At least she'd been spared the humiliation of seeing her husband convicted of the appalling crime. He fretted over what would happen to his babies, his wife, his homestead.

Bitterly, he thought about his nephew whose *confession* had placed the majority of the responsibility for Cullinane's death on Clinton. He was told that Oliver Benson only received a ten-year sentence. Persinger's family and friends in Missouri had rallied to his cause, and had Ellis's case postponed until November 21 so that witnesses for the defense could be produced.

Clinton's only hope was that his attorneys, Trippet and Self, could gain a new trial for him. Eleven days later, on October 25, they moved for a new trial. The court gave them until December 4, 1899 to complete the legal work. County Attorney Duffy was quoted as saying, "I hope they do get a new trial for Dotson so he will get what he deserves–the death penalty."

On November 23, 1899, Judge Napton signed an order that said, in effect, that it had been proven to the court that the defendant (Clinton Dotson) was unable to pay for a transcript (for purpose of asking for a new trial) of the stenographic notes taken at his previous trial. The Court stenographer was ordered to transcribe and deliver a copy–in narrative form–of the trial evidence and all objections, exceptions, and ruling of the court throughout the trial.

On the fourth day of December 1899, Trippet and Self submitted a document which was duly admitted by County Attorney J. H. Duffy. The text stated:

The above named defendant (Clinton Dotson) hereby gives notice that he will move the court for a new trial in the above entitled cause, for the following reasons, to-wit:

1. That the Court misdirected the jury in a matter of law, and erred in giving to the jury instruction numbered one.

2. That the Court misdirected the jury in a matter of law, and erred in giving to the jury instruction numbered 10.

3. That the Court misdirected the jury in a matter of law, and erred in giving to the jury instruction numbered 11.

4. That the Court erred in a decision of a question of law arising during the course of the trial, in permitting the witness John D. Chapman to testify, over the objection of the defendant, that the Codefendant, Ellis Persinger, stated to him at the time he arrested the said Persinger, that he, Persinger first met or got with the Codefendants, Dotson and Benson, at Elliston, Montana; and to which ruling of the Court the defendant then and there excepted, and which exception was allowed.

5. That the Court erred in a decision of a question of law arising during the course of the trial, in permitting the plaintiff, by the County Attorney, to introduce and read in evidence to the jury, over the objection of the defendant, a certain writing from a memorandum book, without proof to the jury that the said defendant wrote said writing, or had any connection with it, to which the ruling of the Court the defendant then and there excepted, and which writing introduced and read in evidence as aforesaid is in words and figures, as follows:

"Helena, July the 31.

Rote to Pa August the 1. August the 1 in Helena. August the 2 in Helena. August the 3 in Helena. August the 4 in Helena. Started back to the gulch the 5. Got to Snowshoe the evening of the 5. Laid over all day the 6 on account of heavy rain. Got to the gulch the morning of the 7. Laid over all in the brush."

6. That the Court erred in a decision of a question of law arising during the course of the trial, in permitting the plaintiff to introduce in evidence a certain memorandum book, over the objection of the defendant, and without any proof to the jury that the said defendant wrote, or had any knowledge of the writings contained in said memorandum book; and without any proof to the jury that the said memorandum book was the

property of the defendant, to which ruling of the Court the defendant then and there excepted, and which exception was allowed; the memorandum book introduced as aforesaid, contained, among other things, the matter and writing set forth in assignment numbered 5.

7. That the Court erred in a decision of a question of law arising during the course of the trial, in permitting the plaintiff to introduce in evidence, and over the objection of the defendant, certain grips or valises, known and marked as State's exhibits 4 and containing matter then unknown to either the Court or the defendant, and which matter was placed in said exhibits by the Sheriff's deputies, and not placed therein by the defendant, of either of them, and which property and matter contained therein was not the property of the defendant Dotson and was not shown to belong to any of said defendants to which the ruling of the Court the defendant then and there excepted and which exception was allowed.

In essence, Clinton's attorneys asked for a new trial on the basis that the defense had produced the memorandum book (found in the vest belonging to Dotson, but worn by Benson at the time of the arrest) and, without any proof other than stating the handwriting resembled that of the defendant, used the notations in the book as proof that Clinton had indeed traveled to the gulch and bided his time in preparation for murdering and robbing the old miner, Cullinane. It was circumstantial evidence at best, even if the prosecution proved conclusively that the memo book and the writing belonged to Clinton; certainly it was not a *confession* as characterized by Walsh when he introduced it into evidence.

On December 9, J. H. Duffy issued a document that stated that the defendant Dotson and his lawyers would have until January 20, 1900 to prepare and present to the judge a draft of a bill of exceptions.

Although intention to move for a new trial was submitted by December 4, 1899 as required, and Duffy had agreed to give Clinton's attorneys until January 20, 1900 to prepare and present the bill of exceptions to the court, it appears that either the decision to extend the defense's preparation time was rescinded, or Attorneys Trippet and Self failed to meet the January 20 deadline.

A document receipted and accepted by W. H. Trippet, the defendant's attorney, on March 7, 1900 dashed all hoped of a new trial for Clinton. In it, County Attorney Duffy moved the Court to strike from their files the bill of exceptions previously allowed plus the motion for a new trial including all papers and pleadings. The reason given was that the "Notice of intention to move for a new trial in above cause was not filed and served within the time allowed by the laws of the state of Montana, and that therefore the above Court has no lawful authority to hear or determine or to pass upon the motion for a new trial."

In either event, Clinton had lost his bid for a new trial and a more lenient sentence–or acquittal–and thus had to accept the sentence of ninety-nine years at hard labor. In the meantime, Persinger's trial was in full swing.

Chapter 11
Persinger's Trial
January 1900

Ellis Persinger presented himself as a study in innocence: the epitome of the old cliche: "If you lay down with dogs, you will get up with fleas." Ellis was from Missouri, where his defense attorney secured over two dozen affidavits from friends and acquaintances. In each, the witness answered a fixed set of eighteen questions. These affidavits were presented when Persinger finally came to trial, after two postponements, in late January 1900. After asking the name and age of the witness, each deposition was similar to that of a middle-aged merchant who lived in McFall, Missouri:

Q. Do you know Ellis Persinger?

A. Yes.

Q. For what length of time have you known him?

A. Fifteen years.

Q. At what place or places have you known him?

A. I knew him at his father's home, near McFall, Missouri, and also at his own home in McFall, Missouri.

Q. When did you first make his acquaintance?

A. Over 15 years ago.

Q. Has Ellis Persinger a family, and if so of what does it consist?

A. He has a family consisting of a wife, and three children, two little girls and one little boy, the oldest being not past the age of eleven years.

Q. If Ellis Persinger has a family, where does his family now reside?

A. With his wife's parents in McFall, Missouri.

Q. Do you know the reputation of Ellis Persinger in the community in which you knew him, and in which he resided, for truth and veracity?

A. I do.

Q. What was this reputation, good or bad?

A. Good.

Q. Do you know the reputation of Ellis Persinger in the community in which you last knew him, and in which he resides, for peace and quiet, and for being a peaceable and law-abiding citizen.

A. I do.

Q. What was his reputation, good or bad?

A. I never heard it questioned.

Q. Do you know the reputation of Ellis Persinger in the community in which you last knew him, and in which he resided, for honesty and integrity?

A. I do.

Q. What was this reputation, good or bad?

A. Good.

Q. How long have you resided in McFall, Missouri?

A. A little more than fifteen years.

Q. When, and at what place, did you last see Ellis Persinger?

A. At McFall, Missouri, sometime in the early spring of the present year.

Each statement was subscribed and sworn to in front of a Notary Public. Among those asked the same set of questions was a druggist, a City Marshall of McFall, an editor of the local newspaper–the *McFall Mirror,* a retail lumber dealer, a retired farmer, a county judge, a postmaster, and a druggist from Pattonsburg, Missouri. To a man they swore they had known him for most of his life, and he was a man of good reputation, good character, and truthful. Ironically, if Clinton Dotson had someone to procure the same type of deposition from his friends and acquaintances in South Dakota, prior to 1899, he would have received similar recommendations.

H. Trippet and James M. Self were defending Persinger also. The press was exceedingly active throughout the trial. Since Dotson and Benson were already convicted, this was the last chance to milk the incident. The reporters described Persinger as "the last of the murderous gang," while his friends and neighbors back in Missouri were depicting him as a "good" man.

When the trial didn't yield the sensationalism that readers thrived on, the reporters polled Cullinane's neighbors and gleefully reported that the public still wanted to see all three men lynched.

A document filed at the time of a second postponement, in November 1899, suggested that his lawyers had just learned on November 20 of that year that Charles Oliver Benson might become a witness against their client, Persinger. They stated in the same document that they had previously heard rumors that Benson might testify–then they heard he wouldn't. Finally, they said, they had been "reliably informed" that Benson would testify against Persinger in consideration for the fact that County Attorney Duffy had allowed him to enter a plea of guilty to manslaughter (rather than a charge of murder) for which he'd only received a 10-year sentence. They believed that without the testimony of Benson (as stated in the *confession* of August 25) there was no evidence on which the prosecution could convict Persinger.

On January 31, 1900, Deputy Sheriff Robinson returned Benson from Anaconda to the prison when he refused to testify against Persinger on instructions from Persinger's attorney. Although Persinger's father, friends, neighbors and attorneys pressed valiantly for acquittal, Ellis was convicted first by the press, then by his jury, of murder in the second degree. He received a comparatively light sentence of ten years, particularly since Clinton received ninety-nine years for conviction on the same charge.

On March 18, 1900, Ellis Persinger entered the state penitentiary at Deer Lodge, Montana to begin serving his sentence, the maximum time of which was until June 18, 1906. At the time of his incarceration, prison documents indicate he was 30 years old, in good health, and able to read and write. His hair, no longer bleached by the hot Montana sunlight, was described as dark, and he sported a partial beard. Rather whimsically, the official description mentioned a dimple in Ellis' chin. Not noted was the fact that he was now a sworn enemy of Clinton Dotson.

Illustrations:

Clinton Dotson, 24 Years Old

Mary Blake, 20 Years Old

Mary Blake Dotson

Clinton and Mary Dotson's Wedding Certificate

Trial #1 Arrest Warrant

Trial #1 Arrest Document

Artist Sketch of Clinton Dotson, Trial #1

Artist Sketch of Ellis Persinger, Trial #1

Artist Sketch of Sheriff Jack Conley, Trial #1

Artist Sketch of Deputy Sheriff John Robinson, Trial #1

Prison, Deer Lodge Montana

Courthouse, Deer Lodge, Montana

James Fleming, aka James McArthur Prison Photo

Artist Sketch of Courtroom, Trial #2

Jury Form Condemning Clinton Dotson and James Fleming

Clinton's Letter to Mary (front)

Clinton's Letter to Mary (excerpt)

Clinton's Last Photo March 29, 1902

Invitation to dual Hanging

Invitation to Dotson Hanging

Artist Sketch of March to Gallows

Photo of Clinton on Gallows

Bridle with Rough Rider Motto

Mary's House with Family

Mary's Youngest Son, Jesse, on Ranch

Mary Dotson and Family Bringing in Hay Crop

Mary near 70 years old.

Clinton Dotson, 24 years old.

Mary Blake, 20 years old.

Mary Blake Dotson

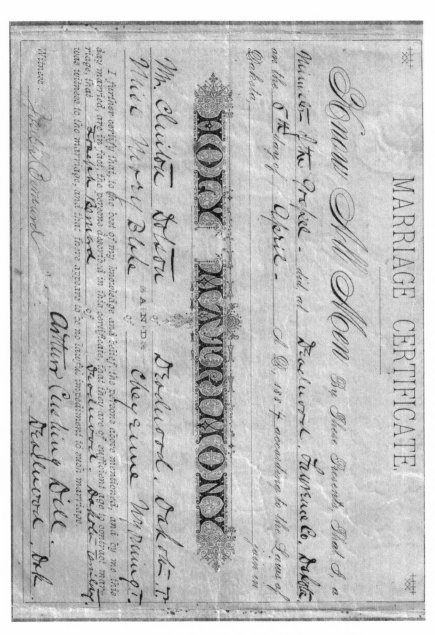

Clinton and Mary Dotson's Wedding Certificate

STATE OF MONTANA,
County of Deer Lodge.
} ss.

In the Justice Court,
Anaconda Township.

BEFORE FRANK KENNEDY, JUSTICE OF THE PEACE.

The State of Montana,
Clinton
Plaintiff.
versus
Alex Dotson & Co.
Ellis Pevenger
Bonan + Jos Lane
Defendant.

Warrant of Arrest.

THE STATE OF MONTANA, To any Sheriff, Constable, Marshal or Policeman in this State :

Complaint, upon oath, having been this day made before me, FRANK KENNEDY, Justice of the Peace, by ___ that ___ the offense of _Joseph Daly_ _Murder_ ___ has been committed and accusing _above named defello_ ___ thereof,

YOU ARE COMMANDED, forthwith, to arrest the above-named _defello_ ___ and bring _them_ before me, forthwith, at my office, at Anaconda, in said Township, in said County.

Witness my hand and seal at Anaconda, this _11 th_ day of _Aug_, 189 _9_

Frank Kennedy
Justice of the Peace.

Trial #1 Arrest Warrant

83

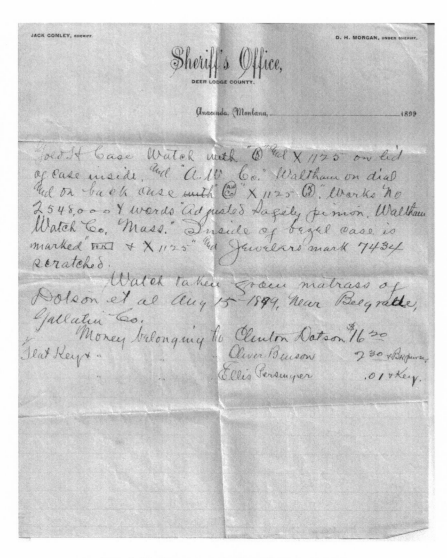

Trial #1 Document showing property
confiscated at time of arrest.

September 5, 1899, The Anaconda Standard
Artist Sketch of Clinton Dotson, Trial #1

September 5, 1899, The Anaconda Standard
Artist Sketch of Ellis Persinger

September 5, 1899, The Anaconda Standard
Artist Sketch of Sheriff Jack Conley

DEPUTY SHERIFF
JOHN ROBINSON -

September 5, 1899, The Anaconda Standard
Artist Sketch of Deputy Sheriff John Robinson

Montana State Prison, Deer Lodge, late 1900s

Courthouse, Deer Lodge, Montana

James Fleming, aka James McArthur

ANACONDA, MONTANA, SUNDAY, JULY 21, 1901.

ATTORNEY WALSH MAKING HIS FINAL PLEA AND RIDICULING THE THEORY OF THE STATE AS TO HOW THE SHOT WAS FIRED.

July 21, 1901, The Anaconda Standard, Artist Sketch of courtroom scene.

IN THE DISTRICT COURT OF THE THIRD JUDICIAL DISTRICT OF THE STATE
OF MONTANA, IN AND FOR THE COUNTY OF POWELL.

The State of Montana, Plaintiff,

--vs--

Clinton Dotson, Defendant.

We the jury in the above entitled cause find the defendant,
Clinton Dotson, guilty of murder in the first degree as charged in the
information.

Ben D Sear
Foreman.

IN THE DISTRICT COURT OF THE THIRD JUDICIAL DISTRICT OF THE STATE
OF MONTANA, IN AND FOR THE COUNTY OF POWELL.

The State of Montana, Plaintiff,

--vs--

James Fleming(Charged in the information by the name of James McArthur,)
Defendant.

We the jury in the above entitled cause find the above named defendant, James Fleming, guilty of murder in the first degree.

Earnest P Schumaker
Foreman.

Jury Forms Condemning Clinton Dotson
and James Fleming

Clinton's Letter to Mary (front)

Excerpts from Clinton's letter to Mary

95

Clinton's Last Photo March 29, 1902

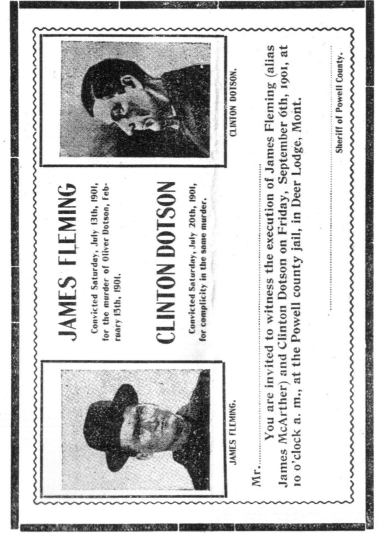

JAMES FLEMING

Convicted Saturday, July 13th, 1901, for the murder of Oliver Dotson, February 15th, 1901.

CLINTON DOTSON

Convicted Saturday, July 20th, 1901, for complicity in the same murder.

CLINTON DOTSON.

JAMES FLEMING.

Mr..................... You are invited to witness the execution of James Fleming (alias James McArther) and Clinton Dotson on Friday, September 6th, 1901, at 10 o'clock a. m., at the Powell county jail, in Deer Lodge, Mont.

.... Sheriff of Powell County.

September 4, 1901, The Silver State: facsimile of the invitation to the hanging.

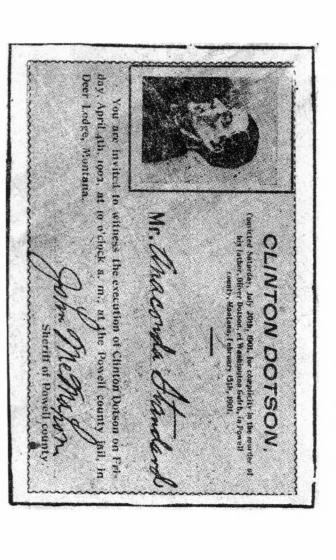

April 4, 1902, The Anaconda Standard: facsimile of the invitation to the execution of Clinton Dotson, based on artist sketch.

THE MARCH TO THE GALLOWS.

April 5, 1902, The Anaconda Standard
Artist Sketch captioned The March to the Gallows.
Recognizable is Sheriff Jack Conley, Reverend Martin,
Clinton Dotson, and Sheriff McMahon.

The Butte Miner, Photograph of Clinton Dotson on gallows. Caption: Murderer Dotson's Life Was Taken on Gallows in Twinkling of an Eye

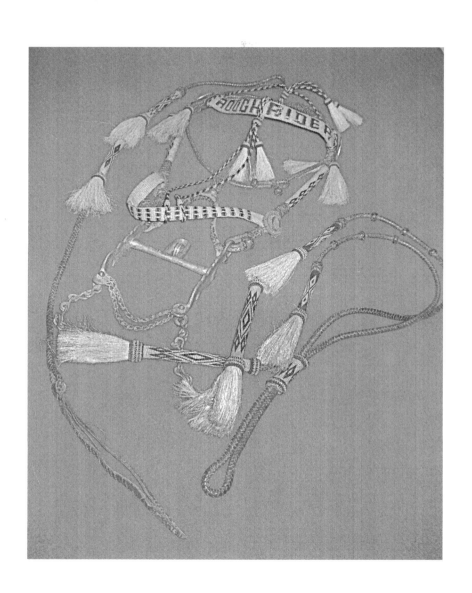

Bridle with Theodore Roosevelt Motto

Mary's House with family members.

Clinton's youngest son, Jesse, on ranch.

Mary Dotson and family bringing in hay crop.

Mary near 70 years old.

Part Two

The Second Murder

Chapter 12
Christmas Eve
December 24, 1900

Christmas Eve, 1900, found Clinton more depressed than he'd been since his incarceration in October of the previous year. Even after the final denial of appeal, nine months earlier, in March of 1900, Clinton still held out hope that his aging father, Oliver, might be able to amass funds to hire a new attorney or somehow secure a new trial. Oliver, visiting his son as often as he could, told Clinton he was still working to get him out of the penitentiary.

Clinton's past profession as a stonemason was to his advantage at the prison. When Frank Conley and Col. Thomas McTague contracted to operate the prison in 1890, Conley started an ambitious program of building that was still in force in the mid-1930s. During Clinton's stay, the brick cell house, built in 1896, was only one of the buildings envisioned by Warden Conley. The years between 1890 and 1921 saw the bulk of the physical plant constructed.

Clinton plied his trade during the day; at night and on Sundays, he plaited bridles from horsehair and finely cut leather, held together with intricately hammered silver pieces for decoration. The handmade bridles were, for Clinton's family, as well as other prisoner's families, a source of income. The public was quick to support the raffles held to sell the bridles, and the money found its way to the prisoners, then to their families. Clinton sent his bridles to Mary with instructions to have the older boys raffle them off in South Dakota. At times, working with the stone or on the bridles, he almost forgot his surroundings.

Christmas Eve wasn't such an easy time to forget his predicament, however. He'd received a heart-wrenching letter from Mary. She was struggling against terrible odds to keep her children fed. She said a charity wagon had come with food and clothing, but she'd turned them away in dread that, if she accepted, they might try to take some of the children away from her. Pride and fear had made her reject the precious wagon load, and now she faced Christmas virtually penniless.

She tried to inject a cheerful note by telling her husband that the school would have a program and all the children would get a sack with an orange and nuts, perhaps a few pieces of Christmas candy. She told him she instructed the older ones to bring it home and divide with the babies. She asked Clinton if he could get a picture taken of himself for her, then closed with her love.

Clinton sat brooding in the deepening twilight, one with the darkening shadows. His hair now matched the color of his eyes; in his dark prison clothes he blended into the gloom of his cell.

The next day, Clinton saw Ellis Persinger at a nourishing, but cheerless, Christmas dinner in the convicts' dining hall. Clinton sat with Ellis, a man named James Clancy, and two other men known to him only by their last names, Newton and Whitten. The men ate in silence, sullen and reflective. Persinger glowered at Clinton several times, but little was said between them. Clinton spent the rest of the day in his cell, moodily drawing on his pipe.

In contrast, Christmas Eve found James Fleming (who had elected to go under the name of James McArthur) in an elated and positive frame of mind. He was due for release within the week and barely took note of the fact that it was Christmas. With no family or friends, the season meant nothing to him. Besides, he was making plans to improve his fortune. He'd spent over half a year as Clinton Dotson's cell mate, and had come to know many of the details of Clinton's life, including pertinent facts relating to Clinton's father, Oliver Dotson. James had decided to pay the old man a visit when he was released.

Oliver Dotson spent a particularly lonely Christmas Eve in his small log cabin in Washington Gulch. He sorely missed his late wife, Sarah, and holidays at their family home in Spearfish,

South Dakota. It had been different a few years back. Then, he'd preferred the freedom of a pseudo-bachelor existence, and was often absent from the family home. Sarah hadn't shared his enthusiasm, as evident in a letter she wrote to her brother, Eli, in 1891, "Oliver is hardly ever home. He stays in Deadwood most of the time. It is too tame in Spearfish for him."

Eventually, he'd opted to live in the mining gulches of Montana, while Sarah chose the comfort of her own house and the pleasure of her grandchildren's company. But, until her death in 1898, they'd always spent the Christmas season together.

Oliver, spending his second Christmas without her, felt empty and alone. He'd visited his son, Clinton, at the penitentiary a short time before, but felt helpless in the face of Clinton's need. There was little he could do. Still, years of habit prompted him to assume a paternal role and promise assistance. A sorry state his son had come to, he reflected, as he stirred the coals in the stove and heated his supper.

Captain Oliver Dotson was seventy years old, and decades of hard labor had taken their toll, physically and mentally. He spent less time prospecting now, often just going out for a few hours and walking along a creek bank or looking at abandoned placer mining operations. Most often, he reflected on the past. His main concern now was keeping a good, hot fire burning in the stove so the arthritis he felt gripping his joints would subside in the warmth. Frequently, his thoughts turned inward and concentrated on his physical comfort and survival.

When the loneliness overwhelmed him, he would make a trip to Helena and sit in the saloons where he drank little, but spent a few dollars on others so that he could buy their company and companionship for a time. He was fair game for James Fleming.

Chapter 13
Fleming Released
December 30, 1900

James Fleming (aka James McArthur), Clinton's cell mate, gained release from the old Montana Territorial Prison in Deer Lodge on December 30, 1900.

James was in his early thirties, though often described as older in newspapers and circulars. He was 5 feet, 8 inches tall and weighed 155 pounds. His sandy complexion was topped with dark-red hair. His features were coarse; his forehead was low, his nose large and very flat, his mouth outsized. When he parted his lips, his teeth were revealed to be badly decayed and partially missing. His head was large and balanced on a long neck. A bristly red beard covered a square chin. Tiny ears and hollow cheeks completed the image. A prison photograph shows him with eyes downcast, like a bellicose prizefighter who has lost his match.

Fleming had a record. He'd been previously incarcerated in Lewis and Clark County, Montana, on a charge of grand larceny for which he'd received a five-year sentence on June 29, 1892. Pardoned on February 27, 1896, he was back in prison on a one-year sentence the next year. This time he pardoned himself by escaping, but was soon apprehended and given a six-year sentence, starting on May 9, 1898.

He appealed and won another pardon, this time with the consent of the prison officials. When he was released at the end of December 1900, he made directly for Washington Gulch, north and slightly east of Deer Lodge, and registered at a hotel in the nearby hamlet of Avon, under the name of J. J. Murray. Mr.

Glover, the hotel keeper, would later recall the ex-convict's unattractive face and unkempt appearance.

He only stayed at the hotel in Avon until after dinner, then left for Oliver Dotson's cabin in Washington Gulch. Once there, it was a simple matter to ingratiate himself with Oliver.

Oliver had felt poorly ever since Christmas, and feared being alone. He often voiced concern over what would happen if he became ill or took a disabling fall. After Cullinane's murder in 1899, Oliver moved to Washington Gulch, but never became friendly with his neighbors. Oliver frequently said he should have stayed in American Gulch, in his first cabin, but his son had given him a bad name. He was aware of the contempt his neighbors in American Gulch felt toward him over Clinton's part in the crime; it made it hard for him to hold up his head. Even though he'd moved to a new location, he could still sense the wariness of the scattered residents of the gulch.

As he huddled close to his fire, brooding on the future, a hard rapping on the front door violated the late night stillness. Painfully, he pulled himself erect and admitted a young man, dressed in a gray suit of clothes, a cap pulled low over his short forehead. Shivering, the man identified himself as a former cellmate and good friend of Oliver's son, Clinton, and said he wanted to visit the old man and keep him company through the worst part of the winter. Oliver welcomed him into the warmth of the room, vaguely remembering Clinton mentioning the man.

The presence of another person in the cabin cheered Oliver, and he began shrugging off some of the clinging anxiety he'd felt for the last week and a half. It wasn't as good as having his son with him, but Fleming continued to emphasize his relationship with Clinton. The convict seemed to be a bridge between Oliver and his son.

Although Oliver's mind was still sharp, he'd gradually sunk into an emotional senility that caused him to grieve over Clinton's plight for long hours at a time. The energetic visitor lifted Oliver into a more optimistic frame of mind. Oliver, feeling alienated from former friends and acquaintances, and grateful for companionship, responded with generosity and warmth. He adopted a tolerant, fatherly attitude toward James.

Oliver made a trip to the general store in Avon the next day with Fleming. He enjoyed the outing, and resolved to spend more time away from his lonely cabin, Oliver made plans to spend a few days in Helena. For some years, he had hugely enjoyed watching the state legislature in session, and decided to attend the opening meeting in Helena the first week of January, a meeting he'd all but decided to forego until the younger man had arrived and invigorated him.

James was glad to go to Helena with the old man; he was eager to taste life and socialize after his latest stint in the penitentiary. Also, he thought the old man would pay for the trip. On January 5, at the noon hour, Oliver purchased tickets for them from the station agent, Mr. Bacon, at Avon. They visited for a while, then sat waiting for the train which was running late. Once in Helena, Oliver rented a room, then took James for a stroll. James, however, was eager to do more than sightsee and persuaded the elderly man to take him out for drinks and female companionship.

Oliver, still enjoying the lenient *father* role, agreed and arranged to cash a check to finance their stay in Helena. On January 6, he asked George Ingram, a longtime resident of Helena and an acquaintance of Oliver's since 1876, to identify him at the American National Bank so he could cash a check. Mr. Ingram agreed, and Oliver cashed a check, according to Mr. Ingram's memory, of approximately $161.00. Ingram noticed the unsightly stranger standing nearby. Oliver told Ingram that Fleming was a witness he'd brought along to the land office to "prove up" on some ground.

According to two female witnesses who would later testify against Fleming and Clinton Dotson at their trials, Fleming revealed his plans to them the night of January 7, 1901.

Becky Ferris, an employee of a Helena whorehouse and drinking establishment, said she'd first met James Fleming when Oliver and James, unknown to her by name at the time, came into the house where she worked. Fleming and the old man had sat by the stove and exchanged light conversation with some of the girls. Becky went over and sat by Oliver, throwing him an inquiring glance.

"Don't bother with me. I don't drink nothing very much," he said. "Go over to that young fellow there. He's got some money of mine and he may as well spend it with you as anybody else."

Becky then took Fleming into the parlor and left the old man sitting there. She wouldn't have paid any attention to the old man at all, if she hadn't spotted a weasel skin that appealed to her.

"Could you give that weasel skin to me?" she asked.

"No," Oliver had replied, "but I will give you one the next time I come to Helena."

She sat with Fleming, drinking beer for over an hour in the parlor. Suddenly he said, "Do you see that old son-of-a-bitch over there?"

"Yes," she replied, glancing toward Oliver.

"What do you think the old son-of-a-bitch done?" he inquired belligerently.

"I don't know," she replied honestly.

"He turned State's evidence on his own son and sent him to prison for life and I am going to kill the old son-of-a-bitch and when I do they will go free," he said vehemently.

Becky was uncomfortable with the change in the man sitting near her and didn't ask him who was going free; she was relieved when he turned the conversation to his plans.

"I've got good placer mines at Avon. I'm going up there after a while, as soon as I get some money."

Again Becky didn't ask for more information. In a town where the location of a mine was worth a man's life, she preferred not to hear any of the details. Uncomfortable in Fleming's presence, she made an excuse to leave the room for a moment. She slipped out into the barroom where Oliver was sitting and approached him. Placing her hands gently on his shoulders, she said, "Say Dad, that fellow in the parlor said he was going to kill you."

In Becky's words, "It kind of queered the old man."

Oliver replied, "I didn't think that; did he tell you that?"

"Yes, sir."

Shaken, the old man grappled with the information, then said, "I did not think he was that kind of a man. Tell him I am going home, I don't feel very good."

Becky testified that James Fleming had spent fifty dollars of Oliver's money on her that cold January night, claiming it was his own cash.

Gussie White, another employee of the establishment, had overheard Fleming say he was going to kill the old man and that he was going to kill him for money or property. She wasn't sure which one it was, as she'd only caught the conversation in snatches when she walked into the room with a bottle of beer for the convict.

Chapter 14
Oliver Enters the Pesthouse
January 1901

Oliver didn't let Fleming know about his warning from Becky; he wasn't sure if it was James, or the liquor he'd consumed, which had been doing the talking. Oliver didn't want to believe ill of his son's ex-cellmate, and didn't entirely trust the word of the comely woman of dubious reputation. He spent the next few days visiting with some acquaintances in Helena—friendlier to the old man than his neighbors back in Washington Gulch—and watching the legislature in session. In the evenings, he begged off partaking of Helena's night life with the young man, although he continued to finance him. On the morning of January 10, Oliver awoke feeling poorly and lay in bed most of the day. He noticed that his face was breaking out, but ignored it. Since most of Oliver's features were concealed by his long, flowing beard and hefty mustache, Fleming didn't notice the old man's blotchy complexion.

Oliver, ill and cranky, decided he'd financed enough of the excursion and told Fleming to precede him to Washington Gulch; he would follow in a few days, when he felt better. He talked vaguely of his arthritis and of coming down with the flu and needing a day or so of rest before he made the trip back to the cabin.

Fleming was agreeable: the money had dried up and there wasn't that much he could do in the saloons or bawdy houses without ready cash. He wasn't a fool. An indigent ex-convict couldn't survive easily anywhere in the frontier west without money or a job, particularly in Montana in the dead of winter. The old man's cabin offered warmth, sustenance, and ease.

Fleming had his plans made and they didn't include working for a living; he'd done enough labor in the penitentiary. He cheerfully followed the old man's suggestion and left Helena on January 11. The hotel keeper, Mr. A. C. Glover, recalled during the trial six months later:

I was acquainted with James McArthur (Fleming). I saw him in the office on the 11th day of January of this year. It was at noon of the 30th day of December that he registered there and left again immediately after dinner; on the 11th day of January he stayed all night, registering under the name of J. J. Murray; he came in quite late–it was after dark–and I took him to his room where he remained until sometime before daylight, when he got up and left without stopping to see anybody that morning. My recollection of January 11th and 12th is fixed upon my mind through standing by him when he was registering, by taking him to his room and by the fact that he disappeared the next morning without paying his bill.

The next day, James hitched a ride with Mr. Mizner, the mail carrier who carried the post between Washington Gulch and Avon six days a week. Mizner remembered Fleming.

I know James McArthur or Fleming; the first time I ever saw him was on the 5th day of January of this year when he was going to Avon with Oliver Dotson. I next saw McArthur on the 12th of January when he was five or six miles north of Avon going towards Washington Gulch. I had a conversation with him, catched up with him and took him into my sleigh and he rode out to a place they call Mr. Kiley's Gate, I don't know exactly how far it is, maybe four or five miles, and he then went across the hill towards Dotson's house. I remember these dates pretty well and whenever anybody rides out with me I mark it down. I looked up the dates and found them just as I had marked them down; the reason I marked them down was that he did not pay me for his ride."

118

Fleming had, since his discharge from the penitentiary, literally enjoyed a free ride and continued to do so–living off Oliver Dotson's provisions and burning his wood to keep the cabin pleasantly warm.

On January 14, Leslie Sulgrove, the health officer for the city of Helena, met Oliver on the street. As he passed, he noticed the old man was walking with some difficulty and appeared to be weak and unsteady. Sulgrove took a second look and it immediately registered on him that the elderly man had contracted smallpox. After a short conversation, he decided that Oliver was in the third day of eruption. It was the first case Sulgrove had found on the street. He took hurried measures to see that Oliver received treatment and didn't infect anyone else.

He sent the old man to the pesthouse, where he would remain for four weeks. Pest houses flourished on the frontier and were rapidly accepted as a necessary means of controlling and confining contagious or epidemic diseases. During his isolation, Oliver came to understand that his symptoms of the last several weeks–fever, depression, fatigue, and aching–were due to the disease and not, as he assumed, his debilitating grief over his son. While Oliver recovered from his illness, Fleming was diligently scheming to improve his personal status.

At the trial, several of Captain Dotson's neighbors testified that they saw smoke coming out of Oliver's chimney all the last half of January and the first half of February. Herman Ruther, a resident of Washington Gulch since 1884, said Fleming had borrowed ink from him.

I know James McArthur or Fleming and the first time I ever saw him was when he came to my place to borrow some ink; that was two weeks and two or three days before the shot was fired which I heard. I had a conversation with McArthur the day he got the ink. I was splitting wood there under my porch; splitting firewood for my stove, and all at once, he stood there outside of my firewood and said to me, 'It's good weather to make firewood.'

'Yes,' I replied.

'A man can't do much this time of year but make firewood, can he?' he said, 'I stop at the old man's place, he is got to Anaconda and I stop there until he gets back.'

'Old man Dotson's?' I asked him.

'Yes,' he said, 'I wonder if I could borrow some ink from you?'

'No. If you belong to that Dotson Gang, you can't have either ink nor anything else from me,' I told him.

He said, 'No, I don't belong there. I'm working for Blair and my brother is working below Garrison. I want to write and get my brother to come with his sleigh and get me at the corners, at the post office there. I'm just laying over at Dotson's cabin.'

He got the ink from me and brought it back; he did not keep it very long, only a short time. He said he could catch the mail man and was going to mail the letter. I did not see him any time after that so I could swear it was him. I had no other conversation with this man when he came to get the ink than I have testified to, in which I told him that he could not have ink or anything else. I did not want to have anything to do with Oliver Dotson. I can't exactly say just how long this man did have the ink. I was still splitting wood when he brought it back and did not think he would bring it back as soon as he did. I noticed the way he went after returning the ink; he went up the road from my cabin and I saw him going down the road where there is a lot of brush and willows and I could not see him any further, but I heard afterwards that he did not go to the corner (post office). After the time he came and got the ink from me I seen smoke coming continually from Dotson's house and there was someone living there.

Fleming was indeed busy writing, but not the purported letter to his fictitious brother. He was writing the last will and testament of an old man recovering from smallpox in a Helena quarantine facility. Additionally, he was penning a crude suicide

120

note to leave on Oliver's body that would, in theory, free three men from prison.

Clinton, at the state penitentiary, was also writing. He usually only received one sheet of paper on writing day, so he wrote Mary a long letter, condensing and cramping his normal style to increase the number of words on the page. There was little he could offer his wife in the way of comfort or encouragement. He told her she would have to make the decisions now and perhaps, if the stock weathered the winter well, she would have an easier time in the spring. He was concerned over how she would get the money to feed the stock, herself and the children. He hoped some of his family in Spearfish would help out, but knew she wouldn't ask them.

He told her he was going to start another bridle soon and try to get it finished by April but that depended on getting material. He owed another inmate for the one he was just finishing. He ended by telling her to make sure the older boys split enough wood for her to keep the house warm—that was the best way he knew to keep from suffering from rheumatism. He ended by asking her to kiss the babies for him.

When the weather prevented construction work, Clinton spent mornings working at the prison woodpile in the bitter cold. In the afternoons, he worked on the braided horsehair bridles. When the light became too dim to see, he sat with his cot blanket wrapped around his shoulders, absently puffing on his pipe. Oliver didn't come to see him and Clinton blamed the frigid, snowy weather for the old man's absence.

Chapter 15
Oliver Discharged
February 1901

George Ingram, a thirty-five-year resident of Helena and a friendly acquaintance of Oliver Dotson's for fourteen years, saw the old man the day he was released from the pesthouse. Oliver appeared well; his clothes were neatly pressed and his long, white beard brushed to a sheen. The former steamboat captain had a renewed sparkle in his eyes and walked with his old confidence. He greeted George and told him that he'd been in the pesthouse just four weeks to the day, but that they had treated him very good and the time had passed swiftly. He felt like a new man and planned to return to his cabin in a couple of days.

They ran into each other again the next evening, about seven o'clock. George was walking home in the frigid darkness and Oliver fell in beside him. They stopped and talked on the corner near Ingram's house for over half an hour, stamping their feet to ward off the chill. Finally, the cold became too intense and the men shook hands, on the corner of Main and State Streets, for the last time.

On the morning of February 14, Oliver awoke feeling rested and eager to get back to his home in Washington Gulch. Over the past four weeks, he'd rationalized that his weakness at the onset of the small pox had caused him to get unnecessarily upset by what Becky Ferris had told him. Probably Fleming had been trying to impress her.

Oliver had noted that the unattractive redhead often bragged about his success with women, but Oliver couldn't recall seeing him with anyone except paid companions at the whorehouse. Probably just idle talk. Oliver had heard plenty like it when he was on the river. A rough breed of man, Oliver observed, always talked of killing and revenge when they got drunk. He saw it as a sort of safety valve, a letting off of steam just like the old boilers on the boats he commanded. Better than blowing up, he mused.

He didn't expect to see Fleming again. The man was too restless to hang around an old man's cabin for long. Oliver just hoped he left some kindling cut up and some wood in the box by the stove. He was feeling good, but, at seventy, he didn't relish having to chop logs and split kindling when he got home. He'd left a good store of dry staples at the cabin, and could get more in a few days at the Avon store if needed. He would have to tell Clinton about Fleming's wild talk the next time he saw him. Clinton must be wondering where he was, Oliver worried. It had been quite a spell, long before Christmas, since he visited his son. He decided to go to the prison at the end of the month, if the weather cooperated.

Oliver rode the streetcar to the train depot for his ticket. Just as he was getting on, he saw Mr. Muth, a mutual friend of his and George Ingram's. He waved and Mr. Muth nodded pleasantly. That night, Oliver stayed with Mr. Glover at the hotel in Avon. The next morning, he rode out to the gulch with Mr. Mizner, the same mail carrier who had given Fleming a ride a month before. Later, in his testimony, Mr. Mizner remembered the date, February 15, because he marked it down. He noted, "Mr. Dotson paid me."

At approximately fifteen minutes after noon, Oliver Dotson met one of his neighbors, a Mr. McGillvary, on the road. No greeting was exchanged. Oliver was getting close to home and instinctively quickened his steps. Although the mile and a half trek from the post office to his cabin was over a fairly good road, the patchy snow and ruts made it slow going for the aged man.

A neighbor, Phil Finisterre, saw Dotson half an hour later. He later stated:

I last saw Oliver Dotson on the 15th day of February of this year on his way towards his home at about a quarter to one o'clock. I could not see his cabin from where I lived, but I could see him from where I was; I was working alongside the road. Shortly after seeing him go up the road, I heard the report of a shot from up the gulch in the direction of the house that Dotson lived in. It sounds like a blast; like a shot off in a tunnel that you would hear away off on the outside.

Another neighbor, Herman Ruther, also heard the shot and placed it at about fifteen or twenty minutes past one o'clock. Herman heard the sound just as he was going to work his diggings after eating his dinner; his cabin was two hundred yards from Oliver's.

Duncan Seaton lived three hundred yards north of Oliver. On February 15, he, too, heard a shot fired, perhaps a quarter of an hour after one o-clock. He wasn't sure of the direction, but thought it sounded like it came from Dotson's place. That evening he went down to see Herman Ruther and Herman asked him if he'd heard the shot. Both men agreed they had heard it.

Neither one made any effort to investigate, not did Phil Finisterre. None of Oliver's neighbors saw any smoke coming from his cabin after February 15, but it was five days later before they concerned themselves enough to check on the old man.

James McArthur (Fleming) was more visible. Several people noticed him leaving the area on that afternoon of February 15. One of them, Phil Finisterre, saw a "a stranger going down the road right from the direction of Dotson's cabin" shortly after he heard the shot. Phil recalled:

He was walking pretty fast along the road and looking over his shoulder. He had on a dark gray suit of clothes and a square cut coat. I was 148 steps from him. I saw him go down the road towards the post office at twenty minutes past two; on the road that leads to the post office; that is a little southeast.

Another resident of the gulch, Mr. McGillvary, also saw Fleming on that afternoon. He said: "I saw him on the 15th of February coming from Washington Gulch and going in the

124

direction of Avon towards the halfway house. He was in my sight for, it must have been half an hour."

McGillvary had seen Fleming coming out of some "willows growing on Washington Creek a little over a quarter of a mile from where I was." He stated that James Fleming had been about fifteen feet from him and that he knew him as the man he passed a month before.

Arza Parker and a young man, Arthur Jones, were coming home from a dance they had attended the night before in Avon. Sometime between three and four o'clock in the afternoon, as the two walked casually along, discussing the good time they had enjoyed the previous evening, Arza looked up and saw a man walking toward them (and Avon) some distance away. As they drew nearer to him, Arza recognized him as the same man who had stopped over at his place, the Half Way House, one Sunday night close to New Year's.

Arza remembered him because his hand was done up in a rag and he told Arza he hurt it in a saw mill down in Bonner. Arza, recognizing the man he knew as James McArthur (Fleming), spoke to him in passing. "How are you?" Fleming nodded his head in a short upward jerk to acknowledge Parker and Jones and stepped off the dry track, allowing them to pass. Arza said he was within four feet of the man and made no mistake in his identity.

Mr. Shultz lived in Avon. On the evening of the 15th he was splitting wood at Mr. Stile's house and noticed a stranger passing and going into Bush's saloon; Mr. Shultz was still splitting wood a short time later when the man exited the drinking establishment.

R. H. Van Sickle was in Bush's Saloon that evening and saw a man, whom he identified as James McArthur (Fleming), in the establishment. Fleming, he said, went up to the bar and took a drink and stayed there for a little while. Before leaving the saloon, Fleming took out an envelope and read a letter. Van Sickle stated:

He came into the Bar Room the same as the other men do and took a drink. I don't know as there was anything more strange about him than about others, but I paid strict attention to him when he came in there on account of his being a stranger.

Allan Davis, sleepy from the long and strenuous dance of the night before, recalls Fleming (known to him as McArthur also) coming in to take a drink and leaving before he, Davis, did. He recognized him as the man he saw in the train depot, around the first of the year, with Oliver Dotson.

The saloon keeper, Mr. S. C. Bush, recalls Fleming's visit in more detail.

He came in there between half past six and seven o'clock. The first thing he did in the saloon was to get a drink of whiskey and then took a glass of gin. He took a glass of whiskey and then asked me if I had any strong gin. I would not have noticed him any more than any other stranger if he had not asked for that. I took the gin bottle out and he took a glass of it and drank it; then he sat down. I then saw him reading what I supposed was a letter; I did not see him take it out of the envelope but I saw him fold it up and put it back. He remained in the saloon some ten or fifteen minutes, not longer than that, and went out about seven o'clock. There was a freight train passing through Avon going west but I could not say what time it was, but I know it was before I closed up.

Ed Mix, a hotel keeper, saw James Fleming in Missoula, Montana on the morning of February 16. At about this time, a letter was delivered to Clinton in his jail cell. According to Frank Conley, Warden at the penitentiary, the letter came on February 16 or 17. In it, Fleming told Clinton that he'd been working on a switch engine, had been hurt, and had been in the hospital at Missoula.

Clinton, during his testimony at his trial, said:

I received a letter or communication from McArthur (Fleming) after he went out of the penitentiary. I received it on the 15 of February. I am positive it was the 15 of February because the post mark was the 15 when it was delivered here and postmark was on it when it was mailed. I generally look at a letter to see how long it lays before I get it. The letter was thrown into the waste bucket.

Chapter 16
Oliver Is Shot
February 15, 1901

The cabin appeared deserted as Oliver approached; he was pleased to see the door was tightly closed, windows were intact, and no trace of smoke hovered over the chimney. It was obvious to him that the ex-convict hadn't stayed long, but then he hadn't thought he would. Oliver was nearly out of breath as he covered the last few yards to his front door. He shifted his small valise to his left hand and grasped the doorknob. The door swung in easily.

Oliver sighed with relief when he stepped into the still room and saw that all was in order. He set his small grip down and hung his hat on the peg beside the entrance. As he turned back toward the room, he heard a rustling noise coming from the partitioned storeroom. Oliver started to take off his coat, then, hearing the sound again, took a step toward the back room: it was his last earthly decision.

The bullet that ripped through the cabin shortly after one o'clock Friday, February 15, 1901 entered at the side of Oliver's nose and lodged in his skull. He fell heavily, his body slightly cushioned by the weasel skin in his pocket. A pool of blood quickly spread through his long, white hair.

Phil Finisterre, Dotson's neighbor who had heard the shot and saw James Fleming leave the cabin approximately twenty minutes later, didn't get around to investigating for nearly a week. During the investigation, Phil stated:

I saw Oliver Dotson on the 20th of February dead in his cabin; that was five days afterwards. I saw him by looking through the north window on the north corner of the house and saw him lying on his back on the floor; his feet must have been southwest.

Finisterre contacted his neighbor, Herman Ruther; they went to the house and looked through the window at the body again. Finding the front door locked, the men notified the authorities in Avon. When asked why they waited five days to investigate, they said they had been "at outs" with old man Dotson since the Cullinane murder.

The authorities found the body of the elderly man laying perfectly straight, the legs and hands laid out naturally as though he were simply resting on the floor. All that was unusual in his appearance was his hair, ruffled up under his head, and his coat, drawn up under his shoulders; that, and the jagged hole where his left nostril had been. His head lay on a blood soaked pair of men's drawers (underpants). Several feet from the body, Deputy Sheriff John Robinson and Sheriff McMahon found a pair of old gum boots, a pair of ancient shoes, and a pair of cotton socks covering a blood stain.

S. N. Arnold, present at the time, described the scene.

At the time I saw the body there was clothing, boots and something under his head where he had been killed, and a gun was fastened up to the cupboard and also blood, blood stains, and brains in two particular places. There was quite a good deal of blood, I should judge a quart or such a matter.

The officers found a .38 caliber rifle, with one exploded shell, fastened to a cupboard. Robinson said the gun was positioned on the outside of the cupboard and was secured with nails and a cord. Another cord was fastened to the trigger of the gun and one end was attached to a nail. The end of the cord laid across Oliver's feet and had a loop in it. On a small commode, next to the wall, lay two handwritten documents. Both contained numerous spelling and usage errors The first was a suicide note:

washington gulch montana
i am now tiard of living and i am goin to take my life and
i will tell the peple some thing i will make my confection
in the year of 1896 in October i killed a man in gallatin
County near sentral park and i hid him in the bushes
about 7 hundred yards west of the Bridge on the wright
hand side of the road going east and in ogest my
soninlaw edward cachelin and myself killed old eugene
cullianene. my soninlaw edward shot old eugene in the
head and i shot him in the back i did not killed him for
his money we killed him to get him out of the way and
we though that we wood be arested for it and my
soninlaw ed. took old eugene horse and traveled to
helena and found where my son clinton dotson was
camped and we watched the wagon till my son clinton
went up town and then he hid old eugene watch in my
son clinton mattress for we know tht they wood be
arested and the watch wood covick them and my son
clinton is not guilty of any crime atall and i can't stand
to have him in prison and my nephew young benson is not
guilty and that other man from missoury is insent of the
charg i hope that my son clinton will forgive me for what
i done to him. oliver dotson

The second document, also written without the use of
punctuation or capitalization was a brief will.

washington gulch montana
i will now make my will i will all of my property in
montana and all my backstanding judgements to my
seckent son clinton dotson and the one i have ronged and
put in prison and i will five dollars each to my six other
chirldren at spearfish south dakota this my hand and will
oliver dotson

Mr. Gleason, cell house guard at the penitentiary, informed Clinton of his father's death two days after the discovery of the body. Clinton would later swear under oath that was the first "intimation" he had of his father's murder.

Rumor is rife in a penitentiary and many prisoners will confide one bit of information or another to the officials in hope that, if it proves correct, they will receive favorable treatment. Correction officers file the information in their memory, but rarely act on it unless some incident lends credence to the intelligence. Oliver's murder stirred the memory of the prison's warden, Frank Conley.

A convict, Ellis Persinger, had approached the officials in December and told them of a plot to gain the release of Clinton Dotson, Charles Oliver Benson, and himself, Persinger. Primarily, he was afraid he would be connected with the plot and wanted to absolve himself of any part in the conspiracy. Conley communicated the information to Sheriffs Robinson and McMahon.

Even if he hadn't alerted them, they would have soon concluded that the faux suicide was badly bungled. Either the killer had panicked and rushed away from the scene too soon, or he simply was too mindless to comprehend what a poorly conceived stage he'd set. Quite likely, it was a combination of the two. It was obvious to the law officers that the killer dragged Oliver's body across the floor.

A more thorough investigation showed that the gun was positioned inaccurately to have caused the fatal shot–the angle and elevation of the gun, compared with the angle of the wound, proved incompatible. Additionally, they discovered that someone cut a hole in the partition between the main room of the cabin and the storeroom. A man standing behind that partition could accurately shoot a man Oliver's height, six feet tall, and hit him in the face. Even more telling were the written notes. It was unlikely that Oliver wrote them: he was an avid reader and a literate man.

Robinson released news of the suicide, hoping that the killer would think his scheme had been successful and be less wary of capture. The plan was dashed by the press, who published the facts in the daily newspaper.

The law men knew who they were after, based on Persinger's confidences to prison officials. On Sunday, Sheriff McMahon of Powell County sent out circulars describing Fleming in detail, from the top of his homely, red head down to his sized seven shoes.

By February 27, the newspapers had indicted Oliver's son, Clinton, based on Persinger's information. *The Silver State* reported on that day:

Sheriff Conley (John Conley as opposed to the penitentiary warden, Frank Conley) has obtained from the prison officials positive information that the plot to kill old man Dotson was planned in the pen before McArthur left between Clinton Dotson, Ellis Persinger, and Oliver Benson. McArthur was told by Clinton Dotson, under 99 years sentence for the Cullinane murder, that his father had a large sum of money concealed in his house, which was inducement . . . for doing the killing and leaving the fraudulent confession, which was intended to make out the innocence of the above named prisoners and finally lead to their release.

After Oliver's body was inspected (it was frozen too solid to examine thoroughly) at the M. Bien & Sons Undertaking establishment, Oliver's son, Hiram Dotson, arrived from South Dakota to learn the facts surrounding the murder. When he left, he bore his father's remains. Captain Dotson was buried in Spearfish, next to the grave of his wife, Sarah.

The Silver State also carried in its column, "Notes from Helena," the following news:

Sheriff John McMahon, of Powell County, spent Sunday in the city, taking a run over to the capital, after having visited the scene of the Dotson murder, at Washington

Gulch. He was accompanied by Deputy Sheriff Robinson, of Anaconda. Sheriff McMahon is of the opinion that Dotson was murdered by an ex-convict after an understanding had with the murdered man's son, who is now serving a life term in the penitentiary for the murder of Eugene Cullinane, committed in the same neighborhood about two years ago. All agree that there is no question but that Dotson was murdered, robbed, and that the alleged confession in his possession is a rank forgery.

The search for James Fleming (aka James McArthur) intensified.

Chapter 17
Fleming Is Arrested
March 6, 1901

Minor Berry was a farmer in the Bitter Root Valley, living on the south line of Missoula County not far from Florence. He'd been farming there for four years at the time he received a letter from James Fleming, on New Year's Eve Day. Minor became acquainted with James in Gallatin County, during late 1896 and 1897. Minor had been farming then as well; James had been between prison sentences.

On February 16, the day after Oliver Dotson had been shot and killed with a single bullet, James Fleming stepped off the train at a small station, nestled at the foot of the mountains, one mile from Minor's house. It was quiet at that hour and James set off on foot for the farm house, situated nearly in the center of the 160 acres of land owned by Berry.

James spent most of the next two and one-half weeks with the Berry family. He was there for almost two weeks when Berry became aware of Fleming's status as a wanted criminal. Berry said:

I had a *Standard* which I showed him: it came there on the Thursday evening previous to his arrest and I showed it to him. The *Standard* I had was like this one you show me, of February 26, the same date. I cannot tell where he went after I showed him the *Standard*. He left my house the next morning–the little girl brought this paper home on Thursday evening and I confronted him with it and ordered him to leave my house and he did. He remained away from the place from Friday morning until Monday evening.

Wherever Fleming spent the weekend, he was back at the ranch for two days before his capture and arrest. During that time, he did his best to win Berry over and insure himself of a place to stay. Berry said that he (Berry) had been "crippled" in a farm accident and needed the help. He stated:

After that he (Fleming) did the chores, cut wood, tended to the stock–in short, he did whatever was necessary to be done. The day he was arrested he cut wood at the wood pile, cleaned out the barn and did the chores, whatever they might consist of, feeding stock and so forth.

Why Fleming, knowing he was a wanted man, returned to Berry's and stayed there is incomprehensible. Perhaps he was too unsophisticated to hatch a better plan. In view of the manner in which he botched up the murder-suicide plan for Oliver, it is not difficult to understand his inability to plan an escape.

Officers arrested James Fleming (aka James McArthur), wanted throughout Montana for the murder of Captain Oliver Dotson, on March 6, 1901, just after he finished the evening chores. They took him to Anaconda and held him there until July, then transported him to Deer Lodge for trial.

Chapter 18
Letter to Mary
April 7, 1901

Clinton received no further communication from James Fleming after the letter of mid-February. He was unaware of Fleming's arrest on March 6, and didn't know of the strong case building against him, although he was aware that Persinger spread rumors throughout the prison. Surreptitiously, Clinton's fellow inmates told him that Persinger had told the authorities, before Oliver's death, of a plot to spring Clinton, Benson, and Persinger from prison. Clinton was uneasy about the rumors and, justifiably, worried about what action the officials would take against him.

In the previous trial (Cullinane's murder), the weight of the crime had fallen on Clinton, partially because he possessed neither the youth of Charles Benson, nor the innocent guile of Ellis Persinger. His sense of foreboding increased as the rumors mounted and the inmates appeared to divide into either pro-or anti-Persinger camps.

On March 15, Mary wrote a long and loving letter, but he was unable to answer it until his next writing day. Mary, distressed over not hearing from her husband, spent April 6, their wedding anniversary, grief stricken over the situation. When they married, seventeen years earlier, in 1884, she'd looked forward to their life with enthusiasm and joy, thrilled that the handsome young cowhand had taken an interest in her.

She'd fallen deeply and irrevocably in love with him. He was a difficult man to live with, harsh with the children and frustrated with his inability to adequately support his family, but a loving man–passionate and strong willed. Now, she could only wait out the days and hope that he might be released or pardoned.

She'd been shocked when Hiram had returned to Spearfish with Oliver's body, and further saddened to hear how the old man met such a brutal death. She dreaded telling her children that not only was their father locked away–possibly for the rest of his life–but their grandfather, Oliver, had been murdered.

Mary also had immediate concerns. She'd managed to feed the children and the stock throughout the winter, but it had taken every cent she saved from selling potatoes in the fall. Her concern was feeding the children until summer, when she could begin picking wild berries and selling them, along with the vegetables she grew. The garden was a necessary source of income, but Mary, suffering from rheumatism, dreaded the hard hours of planting ahead. She'd situated the garden halfway up the hill behind the house to insure sufficient sunlight and warmth would reach the plants; however, the hours of stooping and bending were even more difficult on the slanted terrain. Still, she knew there was no help for it.

Finally, in mid-April, Mary received a letter from Clinton that cheered her. Clinton's letter to Mary was written in a tiny, concise hand; not an eighth of an inch of margin, sides or bottom, was wasted. The prison officials furnished him one piece of paper on writing day, and there was a great deal to tell his wife.

Mrs. Mary Dotson
White Wood, South Dakota

Deer Lodge, Montana April the 7, 1901 Sunday

My Dear Wife and Daughter and Family. I take the pleasure once more to write to you and let you know that I am well–hoping that this letter will find you all well as it leaves me. I received your kind and loving letter of the 18 of last month. Was glad to hear from you all and glad to hear that you was getting along so well but was very sorry to hear that L (a son) and B (youngest son) was sick. I hope they are well by this time. I was also sorry to hear that you had the rheumatism in your feet. It must be awful hard on you to get around and do your work. The best thing that I know for that is turpentine. I am sorry that you didn't have a better visit than you did for you needed a good visit awful bad. It has been three weeks since I got your letter. I am sorry that I couldn't answer it sooner. I wrote to G (oldest son) on the 17th and I got your letter on the 18 so you see that I didn't get your letter in time to write to you last writing day.

Well, Mary, I think that you are getting along well with your stock and the children. A great deal better than I could. You said that you had only been out 33 dollars for feed for your stock this winter. Look what I was out last winter and only had three head. Mary, you said in your letter that L (Clinton's sister) wanted the baby and E (Clinton's brother's wife) wanted J (twin girl). Now I will tell you what I think about it. You know that I never wanted any of our people to have any of our children–in the first place they are too young to go away from you. They won't have the freedom that they have at home and they will get weaned away from you and the other children, and maybe they will get attached to them and won't let you have them when you want them to come home. You have taken care of them so far and kept them all together and you had better try to do so hereafter. I would hate awful bad to think that one of my children was being mistreated by someone else and you know that other people don't treat people's children as they do their own.

You said that you had that hair that I shingled off when we was on the ranch. If you will send it to me I can work it. I will make all the children a chain out of your hair and one for myself but tell them to keep their chains until I see if I can work it. It may be too brittle but I think it is all right. Send it and I will try to work it up anyway. I got your picture and was awful glad. I put it up on the wall by the side of A's (daughter) where I can see them all the time. It makes my cell much pleasanter. R (son) and L (son) wanted me to make them a quirt and shoe straps and I haven't nothing to make them out of now. I have no materials of any kind now.

You wanted me to send you a couple of bridles. I have no materials as I said before and nothing to get any with. I have one nearly done now. I have been working on it for about two months. I will have it done this week. I borrowed the materials from other prisoners. I owe now for a couple of bridles. I will send this one to you next writing day. That will be the 21st of this month. It is all hair and will raffle good. There is about 28 designs on it. It is made different from any other bridle that I have made. I made it to send to a man that I used to know in Cheyenne but I will send it to you. You said that you had the one that L (brother-in-law) had up in White Wood. I hope you will get a good price for it. You asked me if Ben had sent me the money for the other one. No, he has not; he has two of my bridles. I got a letter from S (Clinton's sister) and she said that B (brother) had raffled off one of them but was waiting until he raffled off the other one before he sent the money, but he hasn't sent it yet. I can't hear from him. He won't write to me. I wrote two letters to him last summer but he didn't answer them. The last letter I wrote to him was last August and I had that letter registered. I got the registered receipt from him but he didn't answer my letter so you see how my own people treats me.

Have the children see him and let them drop him a few lines and tell him that if he hasn't raffled them off let the boys have them and they can raffle them off. One of them was a very fancy bridle. I would think that the children could raffle off several in Deadwood. They are just the ones to raffle off bridles.

R (Son) and L (Son) wanted to know in their letter what had become of dear old Dan and Dick. The last I seen of them the sheriff in Anaconda had them in his possession. When I was brought here I gave your grandpa a bill of sale for them and the gun and everything I had. He said that he would get them and sell them and send the money to you. But I don't no whether he

139

got them or not. He hadn't last winter. If he didn't the sheriff has them yet. The sheriff comes here once in awhile. The next time he comes I will try and see him and ask him what was done with them and let you know some time when I write. L (Son) said in his letter that he was going to send me an Easter card. If he sent one, I haven't got it yet.

Mary you said in your letter that you had seen very unpleasant things in the paper about me. YOU MUSENT BELIEVE WHAT YOU SEE IN THE PAPER FOR IT IS ALL UNTRUE. Things will turn out different in course of time.

Well, as you know, I have no news to write. I will have to bring my letter to a close. I have tried to answer all the questions that you have asked me in your letter. The boys said in their letter that they was going to the river duck hunting. Let me know when you write how many ducks they got. Ralph said he would like to see me once more before I changed my looks. I would send you my picture. I can get it taken here, but I know that it would hurt your feelings. If it won't, I will send one after awhile. Well, you see my paper is about gone so I will close by sending you all my love and hoping to hear from you soon. Kiss papa's babies for me. From your Husband and father.

Good night,

Clinton Dotson

Send the hair when you write.

Clinton didn't write to his wife on his next writing day as planned. On April 16, 1901, he was charged with murder in the first degree–accused of masterminding his own father's death to obtain a pardon for himself, Benson, and Persinger.

Chapter 19
Fleming's Trial
July 10, 1901

James Fleming stood trial on July 10, 1901. Although Fleming and Clinton were both charged with the same crime, Fleming demanded and received a separate trial–to precede Dotson's. His defending attorney, C. J. Walsh, making his maiden effort, was battling a stacked deck. The prosecution produced no less than seventeen witnesses that either placed Fleming at Oliver Dotson's cabin, in the area of Washington Gulch, or in the company of the old man. Additionally, a John McDonald who identified himself as a railroad man, testified to a conversation he overheard in a saloon. McDonald said,

I saw McArthur (Fleming) along the fore part of the second week in January of this year at the Atlantic Saloon on Main Street in Helena. I went down to the saloon to see if there was anybody there I knew and McArthur and another man was sitting close to me at a round table that was there and I heard the conversation between these men.

Mr. Walsh, Fleming's attorney, objected to the testimony as irrelevant and immaterial, the time being too remote from the time of the alleged homicide. His objection was overruled and McDonald continued.

These two men were sitting there and one of them said, 'Mac, you had better go with me, there is money in it.' McArthur said, 'No, I have got to go to Washington Gulch on a matter of business; I have got to go do a job there for friends that are going to stake me and it is a matter of secrecy between them and me.' That is the substance of the conversation that I heard there. He said his friends were going to stake him for doing this job whatever it was. The man who was with him said, 'What are you going up there for? To get a hole in the ground you call a mine?' McArthur said, 'No, something better.' That is the conversation as I tell it now and I believe as I stated it before.

Under cross examination, McDonald supplied even more damning details.

There was quite a few men in the beer hall at the time I heard this conversation. I am positive it was McArthur because I recognized the picture when I saw it in the paper and recognized him as the man. He did not wear a beard at that time but did wear a small mustache; that was the only time I ever saw him there. I do not know the other man who was talking to McArthur, he was a stranger to me. Never saw either of these men since until I saw McArthur here. I was nearer to them than that gentleman is to me. (McDonald gestured to an officer nearby.)

They were talking in a low tone of voice and when he mentioned Washington Gulch (I had been acquainted with some people up there), I looked at him to see if it was anyone who came from that part of the country. There was no unusual noise there. There was always, quite a number of people scattered over the room. There usually is music in that hall, but there was none at the time I have reference to, none when I was there; they have a big organ that plays, but I remember there was nothing of that kind going on when I was in there and I wasn't there very long.

Nothing could shake McDonald's well-rehearsed testimony.

Becky Ferris, not in the least bit grateful to Fleming for the fifty dollars he spent on her, and perhaps displeased that Oliver Dotson was murdered before he could bring her a weasel skin, was only too happy to testify against Fleming. She related the conversation she had with him when he told her he was planning to kill the "old son-of-a-bitch that turned State's evidence on his own son."

Gussie White, another girl in the pleasure house, cheerfully backed up Becky's statements. Two longtime acquaintances of Fleming's also testified for the State. Their testimony placed Fleming in Helena on January 7, 1901. Mrs. Pat Hennessey remembered the date because she took her little boy to the doctor's office for an operation on that day. Mrs. Hennessey's daughter, Alice McElvor, testified to seeing James Fleming:

I saw James in Helena on the 8th of January and had a conversation with him. He stated that he was going to buy a placer mine and run it and said that Dotson had two sons that did not amount to anything. He said that he could get the mine and that he would come down and see if he could get my father to work for him, and if he could to get my father, he wanted to know if he couldn't get my husband to work for him and I said, "No sir." He was going out to Washington Gulch the day he left us.

The prosecution next placed John Roberts, a convict at the penitentiary, on the stand. He said that he had a conversation with Fleming in December 1900, before Fleming's release. His testimony was devastating to Fleming. Asked by Mr. Walsh to disallow the stated conversation, the court overruled him and told the witness, Roberts, to relate the purported conversation. He said.

The first conversation that I had with him was between two and three weeks before Christmas. We were cutting up some leather and were talking about his case and talking about Dotson. He said he was going to have Dotson out when he got out, and on Christmas Day, in the forenoon, between ten and twelve o'clock, we were sitting on the wood (pile) and talking about his going out and his getting a pardon, and he said if he got out, he would have Dotson out inside of three months. I laughed at him and asked him how he would do it. He said, 'You wait and see; if I get out, I am going to have Dotson out, and after I get the location of things, I will fix him.'

I told him he had better watch out; he would get himself into trouble. He said, 'I have a place to go to, and after I get Dotson out, I am going up to Missoula to hold up a train; I will get another good man or two.' I said, 'Benson would make a good man.' He said, 'Benson! We will kill him for making the statement he did during the trial.' He said he had a place to go down by Missoula but did not say whose it was.

Under cross examination, Roberts simply repeated his statement. James Fleming's chances of acquittal rapidly disappeared after Roberts' testimony. James sat with his eyes downcast, alternately glowering at the floor and the witnesses for the State. Occasionally he would throw a spiteful glance at the jury. Not only was the testimony against him, but his appearance didn't help his cause: his low-forehead and the expression on his flat, ugly face epitomized the "brute killer" that the newspapers had described in lurid tones.

There was little his defense attorney could offer that might save him. On July 17, the jury returned their verdict. They had found James Fleming "Guilty in the first degree for the murder of Oliver Dotson."

He was sentenced the next day to death by hanging. The execution was scheduled for September 6, 1901. Clinton's trial began on July 17, and was underway when Fleming received the death sentence. The State was wasting no time in dispatching the cases.

Chapter 20
Clinton's Second Trial
July 17, 1901

The crowd had gathered since sunup; at first, only a few shivered on the courthouse steps in the light garments they wore in anticipation of the heat that would build as the day progressed. The temperature was expected to reach the century mark by early afternoon. The men came earlier than the women; they bolted down their breakfast and walked to the scene of the trial in the early morning coolness; their wives would come later, closer to nine o'clock, after they had washed breakfast dishes, tidied the house, saw to the children, and put the butter to set or the beans to soak.

They needed extra time, as well, to don their best clothes and arrange their hair. It was, after all, an exciting spectacle and no small social occasion. Clinton Dotson's second trial, this time for patricide, was of intense interest. Although Clinton's previous trial, for the murder of Eugene Cullinane, piqued the interest of the residents of Deer Lodge, it couldn't come close to the drama they expected from this trial.

The Anaconda Standard said Dotson's trial (lumped with Fleming's trial), was the first case tried in the newly formed county of Powell, and, as such, would achieve the status of a national landmark case. The people of Deer Lodge, and those who had come from surrounding towns, were primed to see history in the making. Powell County wasn't going to stand for crime and rampant lawlessness: it was time to civilize Montana.

When the women arrived, the beautiful old court house, rising two stories and flaunting tall windows topped with Roman arches, was surrounded by the throng. Spectators crowded onto the porch, indifferent to the fluted columns with heavily carved capitals, or the classically ornate balcony. A few men stepped aside and allowed the women, already perspiring and feeling the pressure of their tight corsets, to have first choice of the seats in the courtroom. Within minutes of the door being opened, the courtroom was packed and many were resigned to standing throughout the long morning. They had come to see the "cold, gray man" again and were not put off with a little discomfort.

They had been well primed. *The Anaconda Standard* reported:

Criminal history, for neither the United States nor any other nation upon the face of the globe, affords no parallel for the crime that has brought the county of Powell into worldwide prominence even before it has reached the half-year mark in its existence. Murders there have been more startling, more shocking, more mysterious. But never before has there been revealed such a diabolical, cold-blooded, deliberate plot as that which was hatched in the Montana State Prison at Deer Lodge, and which culminated in the cruel murder of Capt. Oliver Dotson.

Clinton had exchanged his prison issue, hickory shirt for the same light colored shirt he wore two years earlier at his other trial. He appeared, to the delight of some women in the courtroom, fleshier and healthier looking than previously. He'd lost some of his pallor and was clean shaven for the court. Clinton kept his eyes straight ahead as he walked in, flanked by his two defense attorneys, Joseph C. Smith and C. J. Walsh. A murmur ran through the courtroom as he came face to face with W. H. Trippet, the attorney for the prosecution. A strange situation to be sure, facing a man who had previously defended him, and now would do his best to persuade the jury to send him to the gallows.

Clinton sat at the end of a rectangular table reserved for the defense, his chair turned slightly away from the jury, seated on his right, so that they saw him in profile. To Clinton's left was placed a brass spittoon, positioned on the floor for his convenience. He would chew tobacco constantly throughout the trial, and reporters would comment on the fact that his lower jaw never stopped moving. Otherwise, Clinton would remain almost abnormally quiet and still in the courtroom. He'd not lost his faculty for stoicism.

If the onlookers had expected to see a furtive criminal brought into the room; they were stunned by the calm, stolid man who sat before them, seemingly indifferent to the proceedings and, from all outward appearances, not distinguishable from the twelve men who filled the jury box, mostly hardworking, stable members of society.

Clinton sat motionless throughout the long, hot morning as the jury was selected. The members of the jury were:

W. Dana	J.S. Turner
Louis Gosselin	John Manning
C. Church	Ben D. Lear, Foreman
Chris Nelson	B. F. Harrison
Henry Sharp	A. W. Sager
J. Bradshaw	H. W. Evans

At 2:30, Judge J. M. Clements ordered a short recess for refreshment and then asked the prosecution to call their first witness.

Clinton's lawyers counseled him and told him what to expect at the trial. Persinger was going to testify for the State and it would be damaging; that much they anticipated. He told his lawyers he had no defense to offer except his complete denial of the charge. They told him that wasn't much to go on.

Clinton was deeply disturbed, but it took the form of a brooding introspection. As a boy on the Missouri River with his father, Clinton had learned to keep his emotions in check and private. The river life had been violent and arduous and he'd seen many altercations erupt because of an ill-chosen remark. Only with his wife, Mary, had he let himself relax and talk of his feelings and fears. He trusted her and desperately missed her now. He hesitated to relieve the burden of his thoughts in letters to her, both from fear of censorship and because he needed to spare her as much grief and shame as he could.

His counsel had warned him of the intense interest in the case. Even with their admonitions, he was unprepared for the atmosphere of the courtroom. Shock and embarrassment flooded through him when he entered the room and saw it packed with people, including a great number of women. They sat, bright-eyed and expectant, perched on the edge of their seats with necks craned to get a look at him.

He forced himself to keep his face expressionless and his eyes directed steadily to the front of the room. Feeling the weight of their curiosity and anticipation made him recall the cock fights he witnessed when he was growing up. He used to wander the Missouri River towns when the boat tied up to off-load. Walking down an alley or back street, he would often come upon a tight crowd of men, and a few women, leaning forward to observe the blood letting. Clinton had always hated it, not the violence of it; that was a reality, but the injury to the animals. He'd loved wildlife ever since he could remember. Mary used to say he worried more about his team of horses and the stock at the ranch than he did his own children.

With a pang of remorse, he remembered that she said he was more gentle with the beasts than he was with his sons. He'd struck the boys, particularly during meals at kitchen table. The older boys would begin squabbling and roughhousing with each other, disrupting the meal. After admonishing them to no avail, he'd reach for the razor strop that hung handily on the wall. He rarely used his hands on them, but they all felt the sting of the leather strap when they became too rowdy.

Thinking of the boys now made pain knife through him and he wondered if he would ever see his sons again, or his oldest daughter. The babies were formless and featureless in his mind, but he sorely missed his older children who wrote to him. An

Easter card, sent to him by his third born son when he was eleven years old, had become worn and frayed from his constant handling. He finally fastened it to the wall of his cell.

When the court convened from the brief recess, even more people crowded into the room. As the State saw no reason to allow the jury time to develop doubts as to Clinton Dotson's guilt, they put the strongest and most devastating witness on the stand immediately: Ellis Persinger.

Even in his prison garments, Ellis Persinger managed to look fresh-faced and innocent. He settled his tall, well-built body into the witness chair and turned toward the jury, giving them a full dose of his clear, blue eyes and dimpled chin. He began his testimony with an air of righteous indignity.

County Attorney J. M. Simpson strode confidently forth to begin the examination. Persinger acknowledged his identity, stated he "lived in" the state prison, and said he knew the defendants, Clinton Dotson, and James McArthur (Fleming). He said that he'd not been acquainted with Oliver Dotson in his lifetime, but had seen him. He then gave the crowd what they had come to hear–verification of the dark plot conceived by the "unnatural son" of the murdered man.

I have had conversations with Clinton Dotson. The first conversation that I had with him in reference to James McArthur (Fleming) doing something for him took place between the first and 8th of September 1900. He told me that McArthur was going up there to murder his father, and that he would be found dead, supposed to have committed suicide, with a confession on him stating that he and Ed Cachelin had killed old man Cullinane who was murdered up there in 1899. He said they was going to fix the confession so that he took the watch to Helena, and fixed it in the mattress and also the memorandum book; they was going to have that in it too; that we would all be out of the penitentiary after it; that people would think he'd committed suicide and made a confession of the murder of Eugene Cullinane. I told him McArthur would not do that, and he said, 'Yes he will, I am making it an object to do that.' I asked how it was, and he said he was going to give him seven thousand, six hundred dollars. He stated he had money buried in Wyoming. I told him it would not work. He said, 'Yes it will, I have done fixed Benson; if they come here and ask him about it, he would tell that the confession he made in 1899 was made through fright.' He said when he got out, he was going to burn Benson to the stake and that it would only take about six or eight hours to do it.

Persinger delivered the statement in a slow, clear voice. A collective gasp echoed throughout the courtroom when Ellis said Clinton had planned to burn his own nephew at the stake, and had even calculated how long it would take. A general uproar filled the close, stuffy room as the man on the witness stand confirmed that the chilly, remote defendant was indeed a man capable of the most heinous acts.

More than one woman in the room experienced a thrill run through her entire body. This was the raw material of fiction– better than *The Strange Case of Dr. Jekyll and Mr. Hyde*. Imaginations were fired, and the spectators leaned forward to catch every word Ellis uttered. Persinger continued describing why Clinton planned to incinerate his young relative. "He claimed he would do that because of his making that confession. That was about all that was said at that time."

Simpson waited for the judge to bring order to the courtroom, then asked Persinger when he'd next had a conversation with the defendant.

I did not have any other conversation about this same subject until after the old man, Dotson, was killed; that was on the 24th day of February. He said then that we would all be out of there in a short time; that McArthur had done it just as he expected him to do it. I had another conversation with him just before the old man Dotson was found; I don't remember the date of it, but it was the same week they found the old man. He stated that he had got a letter from McArthur on

150

Sunday before that and that everything was working just as he expected and he wanted to talk to me as quick as he got a chance. I said I would be out all week but he was not out any more after that day.

By "out," Persinger was referring to the prison yard, the only place the men had much opportunity to talk with each other unless they were celling together. Ellis continued, still speaking directly to the jury who hung onto his every word.

I had another conversation with him just a week or ten days before he took his plea, in which conversation he said he told Benson, that was what you could call a true friend, a man who had done what McArthur had done. That was sometime I guess about the 1st of April, I don't remember exactly, but it was in the neighborhood of two weeks before he sat here to take his plea. I don't remember of anything else that was said in the conversation.

Simpson asked him, "Did you tell anyone of these conversations with Clinton Dotson?"

"I had told somebody else about the conversations I had with the defendant." Persinger replied dutifully.

"To whom did you tell it?" Simpson pressed.

Joseph Smith rose quickly and objected to the question as irrelevant and immaterial, stating it didn't matter to whom he told it. The judge sustained the objection. Simpson restated the question, asking Persinger if he'd "written" the information to anyone. Again, the defense objected on grounds of irrelevancy and immateriality and the court sustained the objection. Mr. Trippet then stepped forth.

"We desire to show this; that he wrote the facts of this out of the Penitentiary before and during the 1st of January and the last of December," he stated, turning to Persinger and asking,

"When was it that you first told this; the results of these conversations, to anyone?"

The defense objected for a third time on the grounds of irrelevancy and immateriality, but this time the objection was overruled. Persinger answered: "The 31st of December 1900."

Smith objected to the state's next question.

"Did you tell it to anyone else after that, at a subsequent period?"

The objection was overruled and Ellis told the jury, "After the 31st of December. I told this again on the 12th of January 1901. I again told it on the 21st of February."

The only real avenue of defense open to Clinton's counsel was to impeach Persinger and cast doubt on his testimony. C. J. Walsh, during the cross-examination, asked Persinger if he was acquainted with fellow convicts at the penitentiary named Grimes, Woods, Suhr, Whitten and Lennox. Ellis answered:

I have seen a man in the penitentiary by the name of Grimes and am acquainted with men by the names of Woods, Suhr and Whitten, but I am not acquainted with a man by the name Lennox.

Walsh pressed him to admit he'd told other inmates he would do anything necessary for a pardon. Persinger stuck to his story.

It is not true, and I did not state during the months of February, March and April, and May of this year, at the Western Penitentiary at Deer Lodge, to each of those men you have mentioned; that I was willing to swear away the lives of Clinton Dotson and James McArthur (Fleming) because I would receive a pardon or that I was willing to testify against them and hang them both so that I might receive a pardon.

After further prodding from the defense attorney, Ellis stubbornly repeated himself.

I did not make that statement during either of those months to any of the persons you have mentioned in the yard of the

Penitentiary at Deer Lodge, either as you have repeated or in substance. I have not been promised a pardon or assistance on obtaining a pardon for testifying in this case. I have not had any conversations with any of the officers relative to obtaining a pardon in connection with my testifying here, not a word in regard to it, and do not expect to receive any favor or reward that I know of.

In a last effort to impugn Persinger's testimony, Walsh asked him why he contacted Dotson at all.

When I went to Dotson's cell on the 23rd and 24th of February, I went there to try and find out where McArthur was living. My interest in it was because I had notified these parties before the thing happened; I do not know as you can call my actions those of a spy; Mr. Conley asked me if I would try to find out and I told him I would see; that was on the 24th of February. I know it was the 24th because it was the Sunday after the man was found. It is not true that Mr. Conley, the warden or the guards at the penitentiary have promised me assistance in obtaining a pardon. They asked me if I would testify,

He left the stand with a set expression on his face, studiously avoiding meeting Clinton's eye. Clinton's attorneys were aware of the force of Persinger's statement and kept glancing at Clinton, stolid and unresponsive, to see if he reacted. He showed no visible signs of being shaken by the younger man's convincing testimony.

The balance of the first day of Clinton's trial was an effort by the State to wear the jury down with sheer duplication of evidence presented by a string of witnesses who testified that Fleming had been with Oliver Dotson, at his cabin and in Helena, in early January and that he'd been seen back at the old man's cabin, alone, during the latter part of January and early February.

Chapter 21
State's Case
July 18, 1901

Clinton spent a sleepless night, and walked into the courtroom on Thursday in a subdued, withdrawn state. He quietly took his chair and seemed to ignore the proceedings.

Not so the jury. They were alert to the tremendous publicity stirred by the trial and they were fully aware of the heavy press of public opinion against the solemn, impassive defendant. The citizens of the area, spurred by the newspaper accounts of the atrocious nature of the crime and the knowledge that Fleming had been found guilty, channeled their anger, outraged indignation, and frustration at the accused now standing before the court. The courthouse yard was crowded even earlier this Thursday morning. Women arrived sooner than the day before, hoping to secure a seat close to the defendant.

A mystique had begun to surround Clinton that would mount during the trial. He physically portrayed all the attributes that titillated the imagination of some women, particularly the unmarried women; he was still relatively young, attractive, and well-groomed. His silent, reserved manner, and prematurely silver hair, lent him an air of dignity that was in stark contrast to the perceived *outlaw* element of the rough frontier. He was both frightening, in view of the deed he was alleged to have committed, and appealing in his vulnerability. Throughout this second trial, women would send him notes and letters, often unsigned or signed, "Yours in Sympathy.

Once the door opened, spectators packed the courtroom. The cumulative body heat was stifling even before the sun rose to full force. Clinton's trial couldn't have been conducted at a worse time. Jurors often become impatient with the long, drawn out proceedings of a trial. The impatience turns to irritability when they are uncomfortable as well. Clinton's trial coincided with a national heat wave.

The Anaconda Standard reported on July 20, 1901, that the entire nation was afflicted by the terrible heat. Kansas City, Missouri suffered temperatures above 90 degrees for 31 successive days; on most of those days, the temperature reached or exceeded 100 degrees. Mortality among feeble, older persons and young children was unusually high. The same conditions of heat and rainfall prevailed over all the drought-stricken regions of the Southwest: Kansas, Western Missouri, Indian territory and Oklahoma. Denver, Colorado was "scorched," with the hottest July since 1871. In Milwaukee, Wisconsin, July 20th was a record breaker; the weather bureau registered 99 degrees and temperatures on the street ranged from 105 to 110. Minneapolis, Minnesota experienced the hottest day ever recorded there.

Montana fared no better. An article on page two of *The Anaconda Standard* stated:

Helena, July 20. This week's hot weather in Montana, following so closely upon the unprecedented heat in the East, has naturally turned the thoughts of the people of this state to meteorological subjects. . ..

The temperature in Deer Lodge had been hovering near 95 degrees, and within six degrees of the highest ever recorded in the 22 years of the weather bureau's history. Given the packed condition of the courtroom, it is little wonder that Clinton's trial was expedited. The jury had no intention of spending any more hot, cloistered hours in deliberation than necessary.

The prosecution called Becky Ferris who gave the same testimony she'd rendered at Fleming's trial. She enthralled the spectators as she told about warning the old man that the young ex-convict, drinking with her and spending the elder Dotson's money, was planning to kill him. Clinton reacted noticeably for the first time when she related her conversation with Oliver; his jaw tightened perceptibly and he clenched his hands in his lap.

The State had again led off with a strong witness and captured the attention of the jury completely. When Becky stepped down, the state called handwriting experts. In 1901, graphologists were not readily available to testify for either the prosecution or the defense; rather, people in the community who had reason and occasion to see a great deal of individual's handwriting were called to analyze–to the extent of their ability–whether a hand was forged. Their amateur opinions were, at best, just that, opinions, based on experience, not scientific study.

The prosecution first called Joe Stephens, a deputy Sheriff of Deer Lodge County who submitted for evidence letters written by Fleming several weeks before his trial. The judge allowed the letters into the evidence as an example of Fleming's writing. They could be compared with the confession and will left by Oliver Dotson.

The State next offered for evidence letters purported to have been written by Oliver Dotson. The State called on John W. James, an attorney, who knew Oliver and stated he knew his handwriting; he'd seen Oliver write his name on three different occasions and had received several letters from him.

The prosecuting attorney handed Oliver's letters to James, and he acknowledged them to be the ones he received from Oliver; one dated September, one August, one October, and one November of 1900. He said he recognized the signatures of the letters as that of Oliver Dotson. James was next shown the will and confession, found in the cabin along with the old man's body. James stated:

It is not the handwriting of Oliver Dotson–absolutely, because his signature was big. If I received a letter purporting to come from Mr. Dotson, in the handwriting that is there, referring to matters of business with which I was familiar, I would not stop to consider the handwriting if I was expecting a letter of that character from him but would presume he had dictated it to someone and would have proceeded on that; I think my attention would be called on his handwriting. I cannot explain why that is. I will state that for a number of years I was employed as a bill clerk on a railroad and learned in that way to distinguish men's writing and could usually distinguish who the bill clerk at the other end was from the writing. Outside of the three signatures I spoke of seeing him write, I never saw other handwriting of his.

James offered little hard evidence proving Fleming had written the will and confession, and nothing that connected Clinton to either. At most, James' testimony merely cast doubt on whether the will and confession were penned by Oliver Dotson; nevertheless, the jury seemed satisfied and settled back to hear the next expert.

Levi Davis, who stated his business was that of working with abstracts of title, was a stronger witness for the State. He'd been in the abstract title field for fifteen years in Iowa, and for over ten years in Montana. He stated he'd seen and examined a great deal of handwriting in that capacity; additionally, he'd occupied the position of Cashier at a bank in Iowa for nearly twelve years.

Davis told the court that, after comparing the confession and will with the letters written by James Fleming, he believed, "These two letters were written by James Fleming, and this purported will and confession are written by the same party."

He admitted, "There is a little difference in the writing, which very likely would be explained from the fact that, when. . .."

At this point he was cut off by the defense attorney who spoke swiftly and loudly, "The witness is going to express an opinion as to the object of the writing, and I think it is not in the province of an expert witness and I think he cannot testify to that."

The court agreed, but the witness, Davis, was allowed to clarify his comments, "I would say they are simply this; that one is an attempted disguised hand and the other is a genuine one. The attempted disguised hand is the purported will and confession."

Clinton's attorney, C. J. Walsh, pushed for further clarification when his opportunity for cross examination arose. Levi Davis provided greater detail, while the jury craned their heads forward attempting to follow the technical interpretation. Davis stated:

> Taking the original letters (Dotson's) which are admitted in evidence to be the handwriting of Mr. Dotson, and the purported will and confession; they are certainly something alike as to larger letters and such things as that; that is so to a certain extent only because in some places the letter "c" is not larger, but in the majority of instances that is correct and also correct in the original handwriting. Certain of the letters are materially different and there is a difference of compactness in the letters in the purported will and confession. The letters are drawn out and occupy more spaces than in the original letters of Mr. Dotson. Take a word composed of five letters, and you will find invariably on Dotson's letters that it will be a good deal shorter than the purported will and confession. It is so in my experience, in the examination of handwritings, that considerable differences exist between the handwriting of the same person at different times, and circumstances, and also when he is nervous.

Levi Davis attempted to convey two main points: the will and confession were penned by Fleming, and Oliver Dotson's writing was more compact than that found in the will and confession.

Davis' testimony was accepted in 1901; today the very ambiguity of his statements might have rendered it inadmissible.

The State wasn't finished with their experts. S. E. Larable, a local banker, was shown the Dotson letters and the will and confession. He testified that, "The will and the confession is not in the same handwriting as the others; the signatures to these instruments are not the same. In the confession they are not spelled the same." He then described various differences in the formation of like letters.

County Attorney Simpson drew a breath of relief and smiled confidently; relieved there was a firm, convincing man on the stand. He prodded Larable to continued. Larable complied. "Take the letter K and the figure 9 where it occurs, and the letter G and more particularly when the letters are started in T and L they are started back further than most people start their letters; that is shown in the confession and the same is seen in these letters."

Under cross examination by Defense Attorney Walsh, the witness remained firm.

Once in a while you will find the same characteristics existing in the purported will and confession as in the letters from Mr. Dotson to Mr. James; they have some resemblance, but, there are certain letters and a certain style of making the letter L that are characteristic of people making the letter one way.

Walsh pressed the witness. He asked Larable, "Take for instance a word where the letter C occurs and state if the purported confession and will, and in the letters of Oliver Dotson, if in both instances they are not larger than the others in a word."

"In some cases it is so; that is the letter C as it occurs in some places.

"And also," Walsh asked, "in what is claimed to be the genuine writing and that claimed to be the forgery, is not the writing what is known as perpendicular?"

"It is a little more so in this letter of Oliver Dotson's than in the other, but it is in a distinct hand and a hand that can readily be detected without any trouble. It is a fixed hand you might say, Men's handwriting varies some under different circumstances and the pen has something to do with it."

Walsh took the witness through most of the alphabet, or so it must have seemed to the hot, sweating jury and spectators.

Larable had only described the general tendencies of an individual's handwriting; but, to the simple and partially unschooled jury, he spoke with authority and decisiveness.

When Walsh questioned him as to his experience, he was even more reliable.

> My experience in the banking business has been with farmers, ranchers and men in everyday life. We often have signatures on checks and certificates that we have to scrutinize very closely.

Larable again launched into his description of the importance of the letter *K* and *R*. He finished strongly with the statement,

> I have made up my mind from the general character and form of that paper and have explained two or three words in looking over it myself. There is just one letter out of fifteen or twenty in the will and confession that is similar to the writing in the letters of Dotson's."

The State called yet another banker, Joseph A. Hyde, whose testimony confirmed Larable's opinion. Neither the defense nor the prosecution made any effort to determine if the ink borrowed by Fleming from Oliver's neighbor matched that of the confession or will; nor had anyone made a point of even determining if Dotson had worked with ink shortly before his death, in that a trace might have been found on his fingers. In fact, as the next witnesses would testify, his body hadn't been completely undressed or examined with any degree of thoroughness at the autopsy.

The prosecution had managed to wear the jury down with the handwriting testimony nearly as much as they had the afternoon before with countless witnesses who placed Fleming on the scene. Concentration on the tedious testimony, particularly in the close, hot courtroom, was difficult and the jury and onlookers alike hoped for something more interesting and relevant to their experience.

The State fulfilled their wishes by giving a graphic description of the murder scene. For the first time, Clinton heard the details of how his father had met his gruesome death.

The State called Mr. S. N. Arnold, who had two interesting pieces of information to offer. He first said that back in January, on New Year's Day, he'd been in Washington Gulch with a Doc Tibbets. On that occasion, he'd gone to Oliver Dotson's place and met Fleming. Dotson introduced Fleming as "Mr. Murray." He spent the night at Dotson's house and shared a bed with Fleming who seemed "restless and uneasy."

Arnold said, "I slept with him that night and I know I did not sleep very much; he was jerky and nervous and pitching around."

After stating how "peculiar" Fleming's appearance was, he said he'd seen Fleming in Helena on January 8 and talked with him. Fleming said he held a membership in the Brotherhood of Engineers and claimed that he could run a train engine. He bragged he could ride anywhere he wanted–at any time–free.

Arnold then described the next time he saw Oliver Dotson, after the old man's murder. He made the same macabre statement he'd made at Fleming's trial.

At the time I saw the body there was clothing, boots and something under his head where he had been killed, and a gun was fastened up to the cupboard and also blood, blood stains, and brains in two particular places.

The description was effective. The women in the courtroom gasped and sighed, sadly and collectively. Everyone could imagine blood and brains strewn about as their minds recreated the scene. Clinton sat firmly in his chair, his gray eyes teared when his father's body was described, but his jaw never stopped its rhythmical motion as he worked the tobacco. Both defense attorneys were writing furiously. Arnold continued with his description.

There was quite a good deal of blood, I should judge a quart of such a matter. The first pool of blood was where his head lay where I first saw it, three or four feet from the corner of the room, where the first pool of blood lay in the northwest corner of the room. The body lay in the front room, which faces toward the west I think. Between the two pools, there was a streak of blood across the carpet.

Under redirect examination he gave further details.

I took the carpet up; that is the carpet which I took up (he pointed to a carpet, previously entered into evidence and spread on the courtroom floor, in full view of the jury) and brought here, and that is the carpet which was on the floor at that time. At the time I saw Oliver Dotson lying on the floor, his head lay right here.

Arnold stood up and gestured at the carpet.

And that pool of blood lay here (he indicated another spot some distance away) and the feet lay in this direction (he finished by pointing to another area). The pool of blood lay in the corner of the room.

Now that the prosecution was depicting the actual murder, the atmosphere in the courtroom seemed revived, the oppressive heat temporarily forgotten. This was precisely what many had come to hear. Clinton could feel the stares of the spectators like hands grasping him as the testimony continued.

John McMahon, Sheriff of Powell County, testified to finding Oliver's body and the will and confession. He delivered his statement concisely and carefully. It received the unwavering attention of the jury.

I am and was during February of this year, the Sheriff of Powell County. Powell County was created about the middle or the latter part of January. I know where Dotson's cabin is; it is in the County and State of Montana. The cabin faces east. This paper is a diagram of the rooms in the cabin of Oliver Dotson.

McMahon leaned toward the jury and held up a large, clearly marked sheet of paper; the jury leaned forward, some few fumbling about in the pockets of their best suits for eyeglasses. McMahon continued:

This (indicating on the paper) is the east door and opens here and is marked "A" on the map. This part of the map on the top, is the north side of it, and this (again he pointed) is the north window and is marked "B." This (he pointed to a rectangular sketch) is a small commode and is marked "P." This (he stabbed his finger at a circle drawn in red) is a clot of blood, marked by a star and the letter "H" and is three and a half feet from the northwest corner of the room and extends right up against the north wall.

Satisfied that they all had seen the diagram, McMahon cleared his throat and continued with his testimony.

At the time I got there; there was a pair of gum boots, a pair of old shoes and a pair of cotton socks over the blood. This mark (again he jabbed at the diagram) here represents a blood stain, caused by the body being drawn along to this point where the star is, and the star represents the head of the dead man as we found it when we went to the cabin and is marked "F." The feet of the body are designated here by the letter "G." Mr. Dotson would be about six feet tall. This here (he pulled forth another sheet of paper) is a diagram of the store room and is represented by the letter "C" and here, where the mark "F" is, is a large pool of blood where the head lay.

There was a pair of drawers (underwear) under the head. The size of this room would be probably about six by ten and about seven feet high. This, marked "D" represents the north window which was darkened by a miner's canvas coat and oil cloth. This here (he pointed to roughly sketched vertical lines) is a board partition, up and down, and a hole cut in the center of it, dividing the store room from where the body was found, and is made out of ordinary inch-and-a-quarter lumber. The hole in it was about four inches square. I should judge, and about 4 feet 2 inches from the floor.

McMahon stopped and, after several wavering attempts, held his palm out to show how high off the floor 4 feet 2 inches was. Several jurors nodded, one frowned in disagreement. The spectators, however, were having trouble following the description and the code letters without being able to get a good look at the sketch. Clinton's attorneys were alert and making diagrams on their own note pads in front of them. Clinton watched the demonstration, but seemed little interested. McMahon spoke again.

The hole was cut in the partition wall. This piece of wood is the board which I sawed out of the partition, and this is the hole which had the cloth over it; I sawed it out of the plank.

With this statement, Sheriff McMahon reached down by the witness chair and produced a rough piece of lumber with a square cut from it. The spectators stopped fidgeting and watched closely; this was something they could see from their seats. He continued in a louder voice,

I should judge there was three-quarters of an inch space between the boards. I saw a gun there against the cupboard which was against the wall in the north store room and it would be about eleven feet from the body I should judge and pointing directly towards the feet of the body. The gun was about four feet two or three inches from the floor. It was fastened to the cupboard with binding twine and nails and with part of the string tied to the hammer of the gun extending to the feet, and had a loop in the string. I noticed the coat which Dotson had on, and this is the coat.

Clinton stirred in his chair and a frown creased his forehead. He grimaced at the sight of the coat; the last time he'd see it was when his father had come to visit him at the penitentiary. He remembered thinking that the coat was getting worn and Oliver needed to get a new one. He mentioned it and the old man told him there was plenty of life left in it yet. Clinton's eyes misted with tears, but for once, no one was staring at him.

The appearance of the coat was a more graphic reminder of his father's death than the many descriptions by the witnesses. Their voices seemed unreal; the coat he knew. McMahon was describing the position of Oliver's body.

> The legs and hands of the body were perfectly straight, and the hair was ruffled up under the head and the coat was drawn up under his shoulders as though the body had been dragged. From the point "H" to the point "F" the distance is about four feet two or three inches. This (he pointed to a small square) is the chair alongside the commode and is indicated by the letter "J." On that commode, I found an alleged will and confession and this is the alleged will and confession which I found lying there.

McMahon produced two more pieces of paper for the jury. Indicating they would hear the contents later, he held up his diagrams again.

> The back door of the house is there and at the back of the house there is a wood shed. When we got there the door was open about three inches. The door was fastened with a wooden button, but you could turn it away if you wanted to with a pencil or a knife. When we found Dotson it looked as if he had been shot in the left nostril. I tried the wound by extending a pencil into it, and it went in about three and a half inches in a slanting direction, in that way (he indicated with an upward thrust).

Several women in the audience blanched at the description and quickly turned their heads from the front of the room. Sheriff

McMahon repeated the demonstration for the jury, several of whom now wore expressions of deep distaste.

McMahon went on to say that when he arrived at Dotson's cabin, the front door was locked by a key from the outside (at least he thought so as there was no key on the inside). One of the jurors asked Sheriff McMahon to describe the boots again. He'd missed that part of the testimony and worried that it might be important.

The sheriff answered, "Those were long-legged gum boots." Satisfied, the juror settled back and then Simpson turned the witness over to W. H. Trippet who was assisting in the prosecution. Trippet wanted to know what had followed the discovery.

McMahon stated he arrested McArthur at Minor Berry's Missoula County ranch on the night of March 6, at about a quarter past ten o'clock. McArthur was in the upstairs bedroom in Mr. Berry's house. Deputy Sheriff Kendall of Missoula County; Frank Conley, Warden of the Penitentiary; Deputy Sheriff Bishop of Ravalli County, and John C. Robinson of Deer Lodge County had accompanied him to apprehend McArthur.

Sensing the jury's interest in the physical items taken from Oliver's cabin, Trippet asked for further identification of the items McMahon had with him in court. McMahon gestured to each item in turn:

These are the gum boots I spoke of that lay on the top of the blood stains in the northeast corner of the room. In the gun I found there; which was a .38 caliber rifle; there was one exploded shell. The gun was tied up there. There was also a saw there which I wrapped up in a cloth. That is the cloth which covered the hole. I also wrapped up the twine which held up the gun, and everything was all together in the Clerk of Courts office. When I found that saw; there was sawdust on it and still is on it. This is the weasel skin which I found on the body–in the top pocket of the body of Oliver Dotson.

At this point, the confession and will were introduced into evidence and read to the jury. Clinton listened attentively, shaking his head at several junctures as though to deny the contents.

After a careful and deliberate reading of the documents, the prosecution allowed the witness to be cross examined. Mr. Smith wanted to know more about the saw.

McMahon replied, "I brought the saw over from Dotson's cabin because I was satisfied it was the saw used to saw that hole out of the board; there were other boards set up besides this board and a crack between them about an inch wide."

"Is that cut made in the board made at right angles to the crack between the boards?" Smith asked.

The judge interrupted. "The board will show for itself." Smith withdrew his question and asked more about the position of the gun. McMahon answered.

This gun was about four feet two or three inches from the floor. The position of the body relative to the position of the gun was that; if the gun had been fired in the position the body lay when I got there; it would have went over the feet of the body; the body lying in a northwesterly direction. If the body had been standing erect where the feet were, he would have been in line with the gun, but it would have been utterly impossible for it to have reached the man where it did if he had been standing erect.

Mr. Trippet, for the State, wanted to make sure the point was made. In redirect examination, he asked for more details.

The sheriff replied firmly, "I tried the string there. I pulled the string which was tied to the hammer of the gun and it would rebound away past the feet; I tried it three or four times."

The judge then asked for clarification,

"Do you know, if he had been standing immediately in front of the gun and pulled that string hard enough to have thrown the hammer of the gun down, and then had fallen down with the string in his hand, do you know if that string would have rebounded?"

The sheriff thought for a moment, then answered, "I do not, but I think it would have rebounded further in."

Mr. Smith then asked for re-cross examination of the witness and asked if the sheriff had tried the string when the gun was loaded.

"I did not try the string when the gun was loaded and do not know what the result would be with the gun loaded nor what the recoil of the gun would be with a full shell in it."

Judge Clements stated, based on Smith's question in re-cross examination,

"That portion of the answer of the witness where he states 'He thinks it would have rebounded further will be stricken out as a manner of opinion.'"

The judge's decision was small consolation to the defense, particularly in view of how much opinion had already been allowed and impressed into the minds of the jurors. The court adjourned for the noon meal.

Chapter 22
The State Rests
July 18, 1901

As Judge Clements left the courtroom, Clinton leaned over to Walsh and asked, urgently, "Can't I just sit here until all them people leave?" He gestured to the crowded courtroom.

"The sheriff is ready for you to go back to the cell now, Clint, don't you want time to have your dinner?" Walsh asked quietly.

"I don't want them all looking at me–they all think I'm guilty." Clinton countered, "Can't I just wait?"

Walsh shook his head sadly. "Just don't look at them, Clinton. Don't let them worry you."

The guard standing near Clinton touched him on the shoulder and nodded at the door. Warily, Clinton stood up and walked down the aisle, feeling the hundreds of eyes on him as he moved toward the hall. Several women called out to him with words of sympathy and support, but he never glanced their way. Once in his temporary cell, he sat brooding and barely picked at the meal handed to him. He drank his coffee and sat back with his pipe; it would be a good change to have a smoke–he got tired of the tobacco he chewed during the court session, but he wasn't allowed to smoke in there. Still, the chewing calmed him and helped him to sit quietly.

It had been painful hearing how they had found Oliver's body. He couldn't get the coat out of his mind; it hurt him to think the old man hadn't gotten himself a new coat. The woman– that bawdy house girl–her testimony bothered him, too. How could the old man spend that kind of money on Jim Fleming? It wasn't like Oliver to throw his money away in a whorehouse, especially to give it to someone else to squander. Clinton smoked and tried to remember everything said that morning.

He was getting ready to relight his pipe, when attorneys Walsh and Smith came to the cell. They had wanted Clinton to hear the news from them, not from someone in the crowd.

"James Fleming was sentenced today at noon, Clinton: he is going to hang on September 6."

Clinton reacted physically, reeling back as though he'd taken a stout blow. The lawyers offered a few words of comfort, but Clinton didn't respond. When he was led back into the courtroom for the afternoon session, he seemed even more removed and remote from the proceedings than in the morning. His exterior was calm, but his mind was spinning furiously, emotions churning behind his enigmatic eyes.

The afternoon session convened. The courtroom crowd didn't diminish as first word leaked out concerning Fleming's sentence. The room was buzzing, and Judge Clements became impatient, calling for order and threatening ejection of anyone who didn't conform. The prosecution continued with the same theme as before lunch, a description of the body. The Coroner was called to the witness stand. A solemn, dignified man, Mr. Nathan Smith, identified himself as official Coroner of Powell County, a position he'd been appointed to just five days before Oliver was shot and killed. Mr. Smith, in response to W. H. Trippet's question, stated:

I held the inquest on the body of Oliver Dotson on the 22nd of February. I found a gun there; this is the gun which I took down from the wall. There was a cupboard and shelving there. The size of the gun is .38 caliber I believe. There was an empty shell in the barrel and about nine or ten shells in the magazine; those in the magazine were all loaded. These are the cartridges which were in the gun and are all loaded, I should judge, with powder and ball. It has slipped my memory as to how many there were outside of the empty shell in the chamber, but I think there was about twelve. I think the size of the bullets would be about a quarter of an

170

inch in diameter and must be about half an inch long. I took the gun down and turned it over to the Sheriff. Mr. Dotson was shot and killed by a gunshot wound in the side of his nose.

Trippet asked what had been done with the body; what procedures were followed. Mr. Smith wrinkled his forehead and thought for a moment.

"I brought the body out to Avon and there turned it over to Mr. Hufty to bring it to Deer Lodge. I had the inquest on the 22nd day of February along in the afternoon about four o'clock."

Attorney Joseph Smith then questioned Mr. Nathan Smith, for the defense's cross examination. The attorney wanted to know about the condition of Oliver's body. The witness testified:

I examined the body of Mr. Dotson but did not strip it. I did not see any other marks of violence other than the wound on his face. We partly examined the body but could not find any other marks; we did not strip him entirely. We put the clothes back on him again.

The coroner was allowed to step down and the prosecution surprised both the court and the defense with its next move. County Attorney Simpson offered into evidence a transcript of the indictment and the judgment against Clinton in his first trial in which he was convicted of the murder of Eugene Cullinane.

Both defense attorneys were on their feet, strenuously objecting. Walsh practically shouted his protest.

"We object to it upon the grounds that it is incompetent, irrelevant and immaterial for any purpose in this case."

Trippet countered, "It is offered to show that he had an object in getting out of the penitentiary."

Before Walsh could speak again, the court, represented by the venerable Judge Clements, strongly overruled the objection and allowed the transcript into evidence. The defense duly excepted the ruling; it was marked *Exhibit 10* and read to the jury. The jurors listened avidly.

The prosecution accomplished a great deal with the reading of the indictment and judgment. Firmly fixed in the jurors' minds was the notion they were judging a man who had murdered once before. Second, the documents served to show that a firm connection existed between Persinger, Dotson and Benson. Additionally, hearing the judgement prepared them for the State's recall of Persinger.

As the documents were read, special emphasis was put on various phrases, among them "did," "unlawfully," "willfully," "purposely," "deliberately," "feloniously," and "of willful, deliberate and premeditated malice aforethought, kill and murder Eugene Cullinane, a human being."

The look that passed between Clinton's attorneys was grim. It was a skillful piece of work on the State's part. The jurors would remember those words and apply them to the present charge. Clinton sat in stony silence, reacting only when they read the verdict the previous jury had handed down. When the phrase ninety-nine years was repeated, Clinton clenched his teeth. The jury studied him with fresh interest.

The County Attorney conferred quickly with his assistant, W. H. Trippet. The slight pause allowed the jury to meditate on what they had just heard.

Next, the State called a Mr. Hufty who testified that he ran the livery stable in Avon where Oliver Dotson's body was stored on the evening of February 22nd. It had been placed in an unheated warehouse until the next day, then taken to Deer Lodge and turned over to Mr. Bien, the undertaker. Oliver's body was frozen solid in the below-zero weather, and not completely thawed at the time the undertaker, or the doctor, examined it.

Mr. Bien testified that he received the body on the 23rd and that Doctor Dodds had examined it on the 24th.

Dr. Dodds, a new resident in Deer Lodge, took the stand. He'd dressed too warmly for the hot afternoon and was eager to get back to the relative coolness of his office. He spoke quickly and to the point.

I saw the body of Oliver Dotson on February 24th and made an examination of the wound in Oliver Dotson's face. I found on examination, a penetrating wound on the left side of the nose in which the nasal bones were partially torn away and the hole was a little larger than my index finger, extending down slightly to the right and downwards perhaps 15 degrees. The wound was evidently made by a projectile or some object which had been thrown or projected, some small object, I mean by that any long instrument or object of any kind. It had a resemblance of a gunshot wound.

I traced the wound the length of my index finger to the back of the palate and the throat; the blood which had escaped had frozen so hard that it was impossible to trace it further. The location of it, from the evident direction the missile took, I should judge touched the spinal column passing the place called the oblongata.

Under cross examination, Dr. Dodds was asked why he'd not traced the wound more extensively. He replied to Mr. Walsh's question:

I probed the wound as far as I was able to. The blood could have been thawed out in time to trace the course of the wound, but it was not done. It would be impossible for me to state with any degree of certainty whether or not it was a gunshot wound, and would be impossible for me to state what the cause of death was from a medical point of view.

No one had been very interested in examining Oliver thoroughly; neither completely undressing him nor thawing him out. He was dead, and that was evidence enough for the State.

As the long, miserably hot afternoon drew on, the State brought various witnesses to the stand to fill out the testimony. After Doctor Dodds, the jury heard testimony from Frank Conley, the warden at the State Penitentiary. Conley, settling himself into the witness chair, leveled his gaze on Clinton for a long moment then stated several pertinent facts to the jury.

He verified that James Fleming had been in the same cell with Clinton for about six months before he was released. He also said he knew a letter was received by Clinton Dotson after Fleming was out of the penitentiary. He said the letter had been received by Clinton on February 16, and delivered to the defendant by Mr. Gleason, a prison employee. He described the procedure of delivering mail to the prisoners, and then went on to say he saw Fleming the night he was arrested at Berry's ranch in the Bitter Root–some 140 miles from Deer Lodge.

County Attorney Simpson asked him to describe information received before the killing.

"Prior to the time you heard of the death of Oliver Dotson, had any information come to you relative to his death and how his death was to be caused, from any person in the penitentiary?"

Defense Attorney Walsh interrupted.

"We object to the question as hearsay testimony, and, it seems to me; that the defendant cannot be bound by the declarations of someone else not made in his presence, by someone connected with the alleged crime, and we object to it as irrelevant."

This time, the court sustained the objection. The prosecution, saving the best for last, now called John Roberts, the inmate of the prison whose testimony had been so damaging to Fleming.

He again related that Fleming told him he would have Dotson out of prison within three months, and then they would kill Benson. The jurors listened avidly to the testimony; here was a definite link between the frigid, silent prisoner on trial and the convicted murderer, Fleming. With the words, "Benson, we will kill him for making the statement he did during the trial," ringing in their ears, the jury was more than ready to pay attention to the next witness. Charles Oliver Benson took the witness chair; he was prepared to again condemn his uncle.

The courtroom was humming now and voices rose excitedly, seeming to spiral upwards on the heat waves that were issuing forth from sweating mass of spectators.

174

Benson had changed little since his incarceration nearly two years before. He was clean shaven, either in an attempt by the prosecution to make him look youthfully clean-cut, or more probably, because he'd given up his attempt to grow a full beard. His face was leaner, and that, in conjunction with the crude prison haircut, made his ears appear to protrude more than ever. His usual blank, dull gaze was replaced with a spiteful, petulant glare. He'd heard rumors of the revenge his uncle was supposedly going to take on him, had he been released, and the young man now cast a baleful look at Clinton.

Clinton, for his part, had straightened up in his chair and sat tensely, apprehensive about what his young relative would say. Clinton had never been fond of his nephew and young Benson's opinion mattered little to him; however, he did care what Benson might say. He knew the spiteful young man had been the prime factor in his first conviction, and was concerned now over his testimony in this trial. Charles, avoiding his uncle's intense stare, defiantly began his testimony.

My name is Charles Oliver Benson. I was Oliver Dotson's grandson, and I remember about the date of his death. I knew Clinton Dotson, he is my uncle. I know Ellis Persinger, but am not related to him. I reside in the penitentiary. Clinton Dotson resides there and also Ellis Persinger; we were there during the year 1900.

County Attorney Simpson handed Benson a paper and asked for him to identify it.

I have seen this writing and received it from Dotson; he sent it to me through the mail there in the penitentiary. The prisoners pass the papers from the cells to the turnkeys and they distribute it. I cannot say whose writing this is. I know I received it from Dotson because he wanted me to answer it and I did answer it later. I received that letter on the last of June I think and gave it to Mr. Robinson, one of the guards at the penitentiary.

"Are you familiar with Dotson's handwriting?" Benson was asked.

"I am not very well acquainted with Clinton Dotson's handwriting."

"Did you have a talk with Mr. Dotson about your release from prison?"

Benson leaned forward, his dark blue eyes were intent with the effort he was making to say everything just right.

I had a talk with Clinton Dotson, in which he told me that we would get out in a couple of years or so; that was when we first came down, and he said for me to keep quiet and we would all get out in a year or two later. After McArthur got out, he told me that we would be out in two or three months after McArthur did, but did not tell me how McArthur was going to do it, and told me to deny all statements I had made.

"What did he say to you as to why you made that statement and how you made it, or what to say in regard to it?" Simpson prompted.

Defense Attorney Walsh half rose from his seat.

"That is objected to as incompetent and irrelevant for any purpose in connection with this case."

"Objection overruled," stated Judge Clements emphatically, without a moment's hesitation. Walsh slumped back into his chair. Clinton was listening so intently to his nephew that he seemed not to notice.

"He told me to say that I was frightened, and that I had been forced to make that confession."

"When did this conversation take place?"

"I had this conversation with him last Christmas."

Simpson asked blandly, "State whether or not you had made a confession previously regarding the killing of Cullinane."

"Yes, sir, I did."

This time Walsh came all the way to his feet. "That is objected to as incompetent, for any purpose, in this case"

"Objection overruled," repeated Judge Clements, motioning Benson to continue.

I had a conversation with Dotson one day, in which he told me that McArthur was what you could call a good friend; that was about the last of March I believe. I was not talking about McArthur at that time, but he was; he was not talking about anybody else.

Joseph Smith conferred with Clinton in hushed tones. Clinton shook his head from side to side; Smith rose and began his cross examination by asking Benson how many times he talked with his uncle.

I do not know the exact number of conversations I had with Clinton Dotson since last December. I am celling on the same side as he is now but was not at that time, and the way I come to have the conversation was that he was in the yard and so was I; that is where the conversation occurred.

"Who else was present at the time?" Smith asked.
"There was no one else present at the time it occurred. Neither Persinger nor John Roberts were present."
"Now," said Smith patiently, "speaking about this alleged confession that he suggested to you to deny, I will ask you if it is not true; that you, yourself, since being in the penitentiary have claimed that you were forced by Mr. Duffy to make that confession and, if it is not true that you made that statement?"
"No sir."
Clinton shook his head violently in disagreement. Benson briefly met his eyes, then looked down at his hands, tightly clenched in his lap.
"Didn't you say," Smith prodded, "didn't you say to him at the County Jail at Anaconda, at the time of the alleged confession, that you did not intend that should have been a confession, and that it had been gotten out of you upon circumstances that were not free upon your part?"

Benson hesitated, casting his eyes desperately about him and looking to the County Attorney for assistance. Finally, ordered to answer the question, he said:

"Well, it was free on my part or I would not have told it, and I don't remember making that statement to him. I will not say I did not make it."

Benson had reverted to his old habit, avoiding displeasure through claiming a lapse of memory. He was aware of his uncle's intense disapproval and the disgust of the State's attorneys. He tried to please everyone.

"It is true; that after I made that confession; that I refused to go upon the witness stand to testify to the contents of it."

The defense had no more questions, but Trippet, for the State, wasn't going to let the jury begin to doubt one of their star witnesses. He asked Benson, in redirect examination, why he refused to go on the stand.

"I refused to go upon the stand on the advice of my counsel," he answered.

He couldn't have made a more effective statement. It successfully turned the advantage back to the prosecution, and offered the jury and spectators a logical explanation: he was advised not to go on the stand to avoid self-incrimination.

The prosecution recalled Warden Frank Conley. The prosecution still wanted to get the contents of Fleming's letter to Clinton admitted as evidence. The defense objected; attorney Walsh tried valiantly, but unsuccessfully, to bar the letter. At this point, all the defense's objections appeared to be overruled.

Conley said bluntly, "The letter stated that he had been working on a switch engine; that he had got hurt and had gone to the hospital at Missoula. He just stated that he was hurt."

Most of the members of the jury looked at each other, perplexed. Why was the defense interested in repressing such an innocuous piece of evidence? Most of them had forgotten the testimony that Fleming and Dotson had agreed to communicate in code, and that the statement concerning Fleming's alleged injury on the railroad would be confirmation that the plan had been carried out in full.

Smith sensed an advantage and asked Conley if it wasn't true that he'd been told the contents of the letter by Dotson, who saw no reason to conceal the message or the receipt of the letter. Conley denied it. He spoke firmly.

It is not true that sometime after he received the letter that I called Dotson out, nor did he tell me the contents of the letter, or where McArthur (Fleming) was. He told me where we would look for him at the Berry ranch, and I had to coax him for that; the contents of the letter was not discussed.

Smith asked Conley if he hadn't, in fact, been in Butte the day the letter arrived at the penitentiary.

"I was not in Butte the day the letter was received; I received it myself and opened it. It came in on the evening of the 16th; I recollect the letter very well."

The defense asked no more question of Conley. He was too well known, too well respected, and too experienced on the witness stand to make any admissions that could help Clinton's case.

Martin Gleason, a guard at the penitentiary, also talked about the letter.

I had a conversation with Dotson (on or about the 20th or 21st of February) relative to a letter he received from James McArthur (Fleming). I went into his cell along on the second day after this tragedy occurred; after I heard about it here; and I asked Dotson for this letter he had received the day previous, and he said he had torn it up and that it was destroyed. He looked around the cell but not a great deal, and I looked some but could not find it. I do not know what the contents of the letter were.

Under cross-examination, Walsh pressed Gleason for more details.

"He was lying in bed at the time I hunted for the letter. I did not make a thorough search, but just simply looked around. I did not know as a matter of fact that it was destroyed, only as he told me and do not know that it might be in existence still."

As the afternoon wore on, the jury members were shifting restlessly in their oak chairs. Some were sweating profusely in the intense July sun slanting through the courtroom windows.

The prosecution called several more witnesses to the stand who unequivocally placed Fleming at Dotson's house before and after the murder. For the most part the spectators paid little attention to them. They had heard the same testimony at Fleming's trial and earlier in this trial. Only one man caught their attention, and drew a flurry of laughter, when he colorfully described the encounter, emphasizing his words vigorously.

There was a man came there in the second week in January and stayed there four or five weeks; I don't know who he was because I never seen his face. I saw this man out once in awhile working and seen him pulling slabs off an old hog pen and heard the nails skreeking; I was on the hillside cutting my summer firewood when I heard the nails skreeking pulling out of the timber. On the 15th of February, I heard a shot fired a little after one.. . .

The prosecution was near the end of their case, but they had one last witness, one they hoped would carry over in the jurors' minds throughout the night. They recalled Persinger–the only one who could condemn Clinton with more than circumstantial evidence and hearsay. Ellis Persinger strode confidently up to the witness chair. The jury threw off the torpor of the broiling afternoon and sat up straighter; the spectators leaned forward expectantly. His testimony was short, concise, and infinitely damning. The State had planned it that way. Ellis stated loudly and flatly.

The statement I wish to make now is that, when I went into Dotson's cell on the 24th of February, he told me, 'I have sacrificed the life of my own father to get you fellows out of here and myself too, and, if you give me away I will turn

State's evidence.' I have not done anything to turn State's evidence on.

Walsh immediately rose to cross-examine the prisoner. He demanded to know when he'd made the admission to the prosecution and why he was now adding to his statement. Persinger was prepared.

I cannot tell you just when it was that I made the statement about this conversation. I was asked yesterday to state all the conversation I had with this man but I omitted to make that statement which I have now made. I have not talked with anybody–only the County Attorney–since yesterday. I have not spoken to either of the contractors (Conley and McTague) at the penitentiary nor to any of the guards; I am certain as to that.

Walsh pressed him, "Who heard this alleged conversation between you and Dotson?"

"There was nobody present when that statement was made to me by Dotson but he and I. Benson was not present."

The defense had no other questions.

The long, hot afternoon ended, as did the prosecution's case. Counsel for the State announced they rested in the introduction of testimony.

Walsh and Smith had the evening to prepare Clinton's defense. The prosecution based their case entirely on circumstantial evidence–and a great deal of testimony concerning Fleming's participation in the actual murder. Clinton had been accused by Persinger and betrayed by his nephew, but not one piece of physical evidence had been produced that directly linked him to the murder of his own father. The two lawyers for the defense, however, possessed little hope as they left the courtroom. They told Clinton to try to get a good night's sleep as he would have to take the stand in his own defense the next day.

Chapter 23
Defense's Case
July 19, 1901

Most of the citizens of Deer Lodge were up long before the sun rose Friday morning. Everyone planned to attend the trial that day. The prosecution had rested their case the night before, and the defendant, Clinton Dotson, was expected to take the stand. The day's spectators, hurrying through their morning chores and routines, harbored various expectations, according to their own desires.

More than one woman expected to see Clinton testify with the boldness and rakish bearing of their favorite "bad boy" hero, as defined in the romantic novelette of the day. Some older women reacted with sympathy, both for the silent, withdrawn man and for his family. They had heard he was married with a number of small children. Some of the men, carefully shaved and dressed, approached the day in a thoughtful, judicious manner; they were interested in the finer points of the law and the machinations of frontier justice.

Others–rough miners, farmers, and laborers–approached the day with a spiteful, vicious desire to see the "murderous son-of-a-bitch" get what he deserved. They had, in many cases, been victimized by lawbreakers in the barely civilized territory and were thirsting for justice. To them, Clinton was a symbol of the roughshod criminal who threatened their daily existence.

To all these people, the newspapers catered in one way or another: reporters described Clinton variously as "the unnatural son," "a brute at heart," "a cold-blooded killer," a "stoic," and, once, as "a remorseful, bereaved son."

In any case, July 19, 1901 was considered a landmark day for the citizens of Deer lodge, and for those who had traveled from numerous small towns in the area. The trial was, besides being an affirmation of the newly formed and determinedly law-abiding county of Powell, a grand entertainment.

Deer Lodge was staying up later this week, with knots of people gathered on the street corners and in front of the saloons, discussing and rehashing the trial.

Rumor piled on rumor. Some had heard that Mary, Clinton's wife, was at the trial, heavily disguised. Many believed that Clinton was going to make a full confession and throw himself on the mercy of the court. Others said that Benson and Persinger were dead men–that Clinton had arranged for other prisoners to kill them for testifying against him.

The town was in a fine state of excitement and having an exceptionally good time. Business was neglected everywhere. The courthouse yard was filled to overflowing, the struggling grass and shrubbery taking a beating from the trampling crowd.

Clinton watched the first rays of sunlight angle through the barred window. There was still a fresh, cool scent to the morning, and it only intensified his distress. He hadn't slept well, despite his attorney's advice. He could offer nothing on the stand that would belie the State's evidence. All he could provide was a complete denial: a maneuver that hadn't been successful at his first trial, and one he held little hope for at this one.

For much of the previous night, he'd lain on his hard mattress, smoked his pipe, and thought about his father and his early life on the Missouri River. Oliver hadn't been a tender, affectionate man; the extent of his tutelage had been to prepare Clinton to look out for himself. His father had assigned him some of the dirtiest, most arduous jobs on the steamboat–working him harder than the experienced *roosters*.

For the first time, lying smoking his pipe during that long July night, Clinton thought of his father as a man not different in many ways from himself. Clinton, too, had treated his boys roughly. Maybe too rough, he thought, remembering when his oldest boys, seven and six years old at the time, told him they wanted to learn how to swim. He took them to the old reservoir on the ranch, threw them out into the middle of the deep, steep-sided pit, and told them to "swim or sink." They all swum, after a fashion, and he'd felt satisfied that they could take care of themselves in water.

Was he like his father in other ways, Clinton wondered? Bitter regret gorged him when he thought that he'd not spent much time getting to know the old man. Now, he realized, he might never get to know his own sons any better either, might never see them again.

By the time the guard brought his breakfast, Clinton had dressed and carefully arranged his straight hair. Fighting off the fear and dread that threatened to overwhelm him, he drank his coffee and asked if he could have a second cup. When it arrived, it was too strong from boiling on the stove, but Clinton drank it and ate the fried salt pork and biscuits provided. He was ready when they came to escort him into court. He'd again conquered his emotions and presented an icy reserve to the jammed courtroom.

His attorney, Joseph Smith, was concerned. He immediately asked Clinton about the argument he'd engaged in with Fleming the previous evening at the jail. Smith heard that when Clinton was brought back after court adjourned, the enraged Fleming, stunned and shaken at having received the death sentence, yelled at Clinton, "You bastard, why don't you tell the truth; do you think I'm going to swing for this alone?"

"I promise you, Jim, I will tell the truth," Clinton said.

Smith wanted to know if that meant that Clinton hadn't been telling the truth so far and planned to make a statement when he was on the stand. Clinton told him, "No, my testimony will be just as I said it would be."

His other attorney, Walsh, an energetic man given to bursts of pacing and a rapid delivery of words, was nervous as well. He sensed that the jury was under pressure, and that citizens and the press alike, believing Dotson should have hanged for the Cullinane murder, were determined to see him convicted. Smith and Walsh planned to put inmates of the prison on the stand who would impeach Persinger's testimony. In this trial, the burden was on them to prove Clinton's innocence, rather than on the State to prove his guilt. They prayed the jury would give the same credence to testimony by the defense's convict witnesses as they gave to the prosecution's convict witnesses. After all, they reasoned, was one convict's statement any more suspect than another's?

The first witness for the defense was Harvey Whitten. Mr. Whitten identified himself as an "inmate of the State Penitentiary" and said he knew Ellis Persinger. Whitten stated:

> I had a conversation with him (Persinger) in May of this year, I think it was, in regard to the case of McArthur and Dotson. I tackled him and asked him if he was going to be a witness against McArthur and Dotson and first he said he wasn't and after some talk, he finally admitted that he was, and I asked him if the fact that they were innocent; that he would go on the witness stand and testify, and he said he was promised a pardon and he did not give a damn whether they were innocent or not; that he was innocent and was going to get a pardon.

Attorney Walsh asked, "Did he make use of the expression that he was going to swear away their lives?"

The State objected and the objection was sustained. Walsh rephrased the question and Whitten continued,

> He said he had a show to get a pardon and he didn't care whether they was innocent or not; that he was going to get a pardon and didn't care a damn and then he left. That is the only conversation I had with him on that subject. I think that was the last week in May. I was on the wood crew. It was the latter part of the week; probably Thursday or Friday during the last week of May. Another man by the name of Cardon heard this conversation.

Trippet, in cross-examination, wanted to know more about Cardon and where the conversation occurred. Whitten answered patiently.

That man Cardon is in the penitentiary. This conversation occurred in the yard at the wood pile along about two or three o'clock in the afternoon and this other man was off a little to one side. I was standing at the side of the wood pile talking to Cardon and Persinger came up and commenced talking about a bridle of his which I had sent away to be raffled and we were expecting the returns every day and when he commenced talking about the bridle, Cardon moved off a little to one side. Persinger wanted to know if I had heard from the bridle and I said I had written about it but had not yet received an answer. I don't know how I came to ask him the question. I just asked him if he was going to testify against McArthur and Dotson.

The jury was listening closely to the pleasant faced convict who seemed to exude frankness. Walsh felt himself relax and gave Clinton a reassuring glance. Clinton, too, was less tense. Surely, this testimony had to mean something to the jury. At Trippet's urging, the man continued,

He said he wasn't, but he finally admitted that he was and said he had a show to get a pardon and that he was going to take advantage of it. He did not tell me that he had seen the governor, but he intimated that the prosecution were going to use their influence towards getting him a pardon; he did not say who.

"Did he mention any names?" Trippet asked.
"He did not mention the names of Conley or McTague or Mr. Simpson, nor the name of any judge, nor that anyone had made promises of that kind to him"
"Have you been talking to the defendant about this matter at any time?"

186

"I have not been talking to Dotson about this matter."

The articulate convict had conducted himself well for the defense. Trippet however, had an effective method of discrediting the man and asked Whitten,

"What are you serving time for–what offense have you been convicted of?"

Several spectators sucked in their breath when he replied, firmly,

"My sentence in the penitentiary was for 80 years–for murder."

Trippet turned and looked to the jury and nodded his head as if to say, *You see, another murderer with nothing to lose by testifying.* Some jurors seemed to get the message. Trippet then asked several questions in hope of establishing a friendship between the witness and the defendant.

Whitten answered, "Dotson and I are in the same penitentiary: he cells on one side and I on the other. The only communication we have is through the guards."

Trippet's last question concerned inmates' attitude over the incident. Whitten responded,

I cannot say if there is considerable feeling against anyone in the penitentiary who goes out to testify against another convict; there is some among some classes of prisoners. They have not made it hot for Persinger ever since it was known that this thing commenced.

Whitten started to step down and Trippet thought of one more question. He wanted to know who had asked Whitten to side with Dotson.

"Nobody asked me to come and say that Persinger talked with me in May. The conversation just came out and I asked him if he was going to testify against Dotson."

Whitten was the only witness for the defense to identify himself as an "inmate" of the penitentiary. The witnesses who followed, either from whimsy or to avoid humiliation, found a variety of methods to describe their residence.

Hiram Woods, second witness for the defense, simply said he "lived in" the penitentiary and had, for four years and eleven months. He testified:

> I know an inmate of that place by the name of Persinger and have known him about a year, ever since he has been there. I have had a conversation with him during this year; it was sometime in February, about the 26th I think, somewhere along there.

Smith asked, "What was the substance of the conversation you had with him?"

Mr. Trippet objected because a foundation hadn't been laid for the question. The judge responded favorably to the State and took a moment to offer some advice to the counsel.

> The objection is good for this reason. In propounding a question impeaching a witness, it should be propounded in the same language as to the other witnesses in laying the foundation and should be asked whether or not he did state so and so. The other side have the right to question for the whole conversation. You may ask this witness the question so framed.

Walsh was still learning and gaining experience; he accepted the instructions gracefully and asked the leave of the court to rephrase his questions.

"I will ask you to state whether or not, during the months of February, March, April and May, at the Penitentiary at Deer Lodge, you had a conversation with Ellis Persinger in that institution regarding the question of the charge against McArthur and Clinton Dotson."

Judge Clements interrupted again, "I sustained the objection to that form of a question."

Chastened, Walsh began again.

"I will ask you to state if Ellis Persinger in that conversation said this to you during the month of February as you said, in the penitentiary yard at the penitentiary situated at Deer Lodge–did he not state to you; that he was willing to swear away the life of Clinton Dotson and James McArthur (Fleming) because he would receive a pardon, and was willing to testify against them and hang them both if he might receive a pardon?"

"No sir." Woods said flatly. A murmur ran through the courtroom. Had the defense's witness turned against Clinton? Walsh understood the man hadn't, but found it awkward to get the question phrased correctly so the man could answer truthfully.

"Did he state that in substance?"

"No sir, he did not to me."

Walsh tried again. "I will ask you to state if he said any part of that conversation to you?"

Trippet interrupted. "What part do you allude to?"

Defense Attorney Walsh was becoming frustrated. He looked at Trippet, then turned to his witness.

"Did he state that conversation to you, or any part of it, or that in substance?"

Trippet smiled. "We object to that as it is an improper question."

Finally the court allowed the witness to continue.

"He did state a part of it, yes sir," Woods stated with relief.

"What part of this conversation that I have mentioned or the statement I have mentioned; what part of it did he state at the time this has been asked you?"

"He did not right at that time. He stated later on that he expected to get a pardon on the strength of it; that was along in April. That was in the penitentiary yard at the wood pile. That yard is situated at Deer Lodge."

Wood's testimony incriminated Persinger, but most of the impact was lost on the jury because of the flurry of objections and the blundering attempts of defense counsel to elicit the information.

Attorney Trippet conducted a short cross-examination, again asking the witness for the defense to testify to his own incarceration.

"I am in the penitentiary for highway robbery committed over at Ovando in this county," Wood stated. Trippet nodded affirmatively.

The third witness for the defense, one Fred Grimes, had a delicate way of telling the packed courtroom where he lived.

"At the present time, I reside with Conley and McTague at the state prison." (Warden Conley and Thomas McTague contracted for, and operated, the prison.)

Several people in the audience tittered at the testimony. "Resides indeed!" one matron said loudly. Judge Clements pounded for order and Grimes continued. He said that he, too, had a conversation with Persinger.

Walsh, primed now in correct procedure, asked him,"You had a conversation with Ellis Persinger in which he made a statement to you; that he was going to testify against McArthur and Clinton Dotson; that he expected or was promised a pardon, and that it did not make any difference whether they were innocent or not; he was going to save himself because he was innocent?"

Grimes responded:

He did not make the full statement to me, but he made a part of it while he was working on the dining room crew in May or April. When he made the remark to me there was no one present. He made the remark that he did not care how many innocent men were hanged as long as he got out of prison, nor who were convicted, and I told him I did not care to have any further remarks with him and I had none!

"Did you speak with him again?"

"We was working at the elevator and he started to talk to me again and I told him I did not care to have any further conversation with him after the remarks he made to me. That's all I remember he stated."

Trippet was displeased with the witness' strong testimony and attempted to discredit it. He asked why Persinger should talk to Grimes about the matter.

The convict spoke clearly, looking directly into the prosecuting attorney's eyes.

This matter was common talk in the prison. I did not want to find out about it and did not ask about it; he spoke of it voluntarily. We were pretty friendly there, but one man came up to the table and made an insulting remark about informers and about a man that would go to work and swear against another man and Persinger called this man over and made some kind of remark to him. I don't know what they were talking about, and the next day we got to talking and that was when our conversation occurred and in that conversation he told me he didn't care how many innocent men were hanged as long as he got out of prison.

"Did he tell you on that occasion what his testimony would be?" Trippet asked.

He did not tell me what his testimony would be. He did not tell me that he told Frank Conley and others that a crime was committed; he just told me voluntarily that he didn't care how many innocent men were convicted as long as he got out of prison. One day they got to talking about what a dirty trick it was to testify against a man.

Trippet asked him to clarify his last statement. Grimes was happy to do so.

There are quite a number up there who are down on Persinger and I guess the reason is because of the dirtiness of giving this case away; that's about all I can say. I don't know whether or not it is because he gave it away to the State. They are talking about it in general up there and about what a cur a man is who would do such a thing. What I meant, when I said the prisoners were talking against informers, is that they seemed to be under the impression up there that when a man voluntarily goes out to swear against a man; that he's doing it for a pardon.

Trippet leaned close to the witness, "They cannot believe that a man could be truthful or anything else without having an object in view?"

Grimes didn't get to answer. Walsh objected and the court sustained it. Trippet did, however, find out that Grimes was serving eight years for robbery.

The Anaconda Standard quoted Grimes as saying that Persinger stated he "Would hang his own mother to get out of prison."

The defense's fourth witness, one Louis Suhr, was even more casual about his residence. He informed the jury and thronged courtroom that he was "stopping over at the penitentiary now." In actuality, he was "stopping over" for a term of five years for Grand Larceny. His statement wasn't lost on the more lighthearted in the spectator section, and the hint of a smile crossed the face of more than one juror.

J. Walsh had his questioning technique down pat now and quickly drew the pertinent facts from the witness. Mr. Suhr stated that Persinger had told him:

McArthur went out of the penitentiary to kill Mr. Dotson and said that he knew he was going to kill him and that this man Dotson here (gesturing to the defendant) was as guilty as McArthur was and that he should be hanged and told me he was going to get a pardon for swearing on them.

"What, if anything, was said in that conversation regarding the guilt or innocence of those men?"

"Well," Suhr exclaimed, "he said he did not know; that he did not think McArthur would do that but, he said, McArthur told him he was going to do it."

Walsh pressed eagerly. "What if anything was said by him as to whether he would swear these men were guilty, if anything of that kind was said?"

192

"He told me if he could convict Clinton Dotson and James McArthur that he was going to get out of prison."

Defense Attorney Walsh said he had no more questions, and turned the witness over to W. H. Trippet to cross-examine for the State. Trippet wanted verification. The convict answered:

"He did not tell me it was a sure thing that he would get a pardon if he would convict these two men."

"Well, did he tell you his testimony was necessary to convict anybody?"

"He told me they wanted him to come up here and to tell a lie against these two men and said this man Dotson here wanted him to testify that he told him a lot of stuff to swear to when he came up here." Suhr replied.

"Did he tell you he told other parties about this thing that McArthur was going to do long before it happened?" Trippet asked.

"He told me McArthur was going to kill old man Dotson before it was done. I don't know whether it was done then or not. That was in February." Suhr continued, "I don't know whether old man Dotson was killed then or not, it was along the latter part of February."

Nothing further could be gained from the witness and Trippet allowed him to step down.

The defense attorneys called yet another convict to the witness chair. They hadn't any other reliable strategy–only their hopes of impeaching Persinger's damning testimony.

Clinton sat calmly and impassively throughout the previous testimony. He met Suhr's eyes once, and tried to convey his appreciation, but was careful not to nod or show friendliness to him. The jury might take that as a bad sign. What he heard them say gave him hope; maybe he could write to Mary next writing day and tell her everything was going to be all right. He didn't allow himself to think about the ninety-six years remaining on his original sentence.

Smith and Walsh were less optimistic. The general stance of the jury seemed the same; they couldn't detect any perceptible change in expression or attitude among the twelve men. There were no signs to indicate whether they were impressed by the testimony so far presented. Drawing a deep breath, Walsh strode to the front of the courtroom and called the next witness, another convict at the State penitentiary named Isaac Gravelle. The defense would have been better off if they had not called him. Walsh asked him his now well rehearsed question.

Did you have a conversation with Persinger during the months of February, March, April, or May of this year at the penitentiary, in which he made this statement–that he, Persinger, was going to be a witness in this case, and that he intended to testify that McArthur and Clinton Dotson had agreed to have Dotson's father murdered, and that McArthur was to do the work and that he intended to testify, and, that it did not make any difference whether they were guilty or innocent; that he was going on the stand to testify so that he could get a pardon?

The witness answered:

I spoke to him three or four months or more–the last time I had a conversation with him I was at work on the wood pile; that was about a month ago, somewhere along about June. I was talking to him in regard to that matter and he denied it to me about coming here to tell anything or telling the warden anything about that or being a witness. He didn't say anything to me about coming to testify at all nor about going into court to make a statement in regard to this matter; he never mentioned it one way or the other.

Walsh tried again and the witness again put forth a denial. Obviously, Gravelle had changed his mind about testifying for Clinton. The State wisely didn't cross examine. Isaac had damaged the defense enough.

One more witness was called before the noontime break. The defense called Herbert Lennox who said he was "confined at the present time" for "jail breaking" for which he'd received a six-month sentence. Walsh asked his set question and Lennox stated:

> I drew from what he (Persinger) said that he would do that (testify for a pardon). He said he could get a pardon if he testified for the State. I cannot tell just what he did state, I cannot remember his exact language.

Judge Clements noted the time and the rumblings of his own empty stomach. He adjourned the court for a noon break and walked quickly to his chambers. The crowd rushed out, chattering happily. The weather was no cooler than it had been all week, but they anticipated an exciting afternoon. Most of the men rushed to the saloons for a cold drink and a bar-lunch. Many women had to make a rapid trip home to check on the children and issue orders for supper. Only a few didn't come back for the afternoon session.

Clinton was in earnest conversation with his attorneys; they sensed that their defense was weak at best and hoped Clinton could convince the jury that he was telling the truth. Privately they doubted it, but they went through the testimony with him, then left him in the temporary cell to have his meal in peace. Clinton ate lightly, pushed most of the food away, and sipped coffee. He lit his pipe; it was a comfort and he concentrated on drawing the smoke through the long stem, fighting to maintain a calm he didn't feel.

Chapter 24
Clinton's Testimony
July 19, 1901

The afternoon gathering of spectators in the courtroom conveyed a new mood: the people were hushed, expectant, somber and just a little fearful. It had been widely rumored that the defendant would make a "clean breast" of the whole affair. Some expected a dramatic emotional breakdown by Dotson. After all, how could the man face his accusers, the jury, and the judge and not tell the truth and beg for mercy? Others believed Clinton would behave like the stereotypic frontier outlaw–crude and brash on the stand.

His attorneys would have preferred either to the colorless denial they expected him to make. Clinton was too introspective and uncommunicative for his own good. If he had broken his reserve and showed the human side of his personality, let the jury glimpse the man inside the cold, gray shell, then he might have touched them, might have made them pity this father of nine children who stood accused of that most heinous of crimes–patricide.

But Clinton simply wasn't made that way. His temperament had been determined during his formative years on the Missouri River, where he'd learned survival was enhanced by keeping one's mouth shut, by not revealing one's thoughts, Helping his father run the freight line hadn't enlarged his sensitivity to others, as the work was long, demanding, and hardly the place to discuss emotions or perceptions.

Clinton had, in short, never had anyone to talk to about how he thought, or what he felt, other than his wife Mary. He worshiped her and, in her, had found the only total acceptance he ever knew. To the rest of the world, even to his own children, he was an abrupt, stern, often unrelenting man. To Mary, he was the dreamer, the boy who appreciated the song of the birds and the scent of wild flowers. Even as Clinton had grown more lined and worn, and Mary had become hopelessly overweight for her five-foot, three-inch frame, the joy in each other hadn't diminished.

Unfortunately, the jury and the spectators couldn't begin to conceive of the twisting grief Clinton felt over what the trial and his prison term was doing to Mary. His brothers and sisters hadn't come to see him in prison, nor had they contributed anything to his defense—either through word, deed or hard cash. Except for his relationship with Mary, Clinton had never been close to anyone and now, before a jury of his peers, had no way of conveying his own humanity.

After being duly sworn, Clinton identified himself as the defendant and the son of Oliver Dotson. C. J. Walsh was conducting the questions for the defense. He asked Clinton to describe his relationship with Fleming. Clinton replied in an even tone:

> I have been in the penitentiary two years the 17th of next month, but during that time I was taken out for six weeks. I was taken out in August 1899, and brought back on the 14th day of October, after my conviction. Part of the time I was in was before my trial for the murder of Eugene Cullinane. I have been acquainted with James McArthur, or Fleming as he is called, for about a year or a little over; he was a cellmate of mine for about six months in the penitentiary. I have had eight other cellmates. He was my cellmate for the latter part of June of last year until the 29th of December of last year. During the time he was in my cell we never had any talk or conversation relative to Oliver Dotson.

Walsh leaned close to Clinton, his voice urgent. "I will ask you to state, Mr. Dotson, whether you or he ever had any conversation, statement or agreement or otherwise in relation to anything that should be done with Oliver Dotson, so as to release yourself, Benson and Persinger from the penitentiary?"

"No sir, we did not." Clinton replied emphatically.

"I will ask you to state if at the time McArthur left the penitentiary, or prior to that time, you knew that he was to have any agreement with anyone in regard to doing anything to release you from the penitentiary, or anything in relation to your father, Oliver Dotson?"

Clinton spoke directly to his attorney. "No sir. The first intimation I had of the death of Oliver Dotson was on the 22nd day of February; I got the information from Mr. Gleason; he is the cell house guard and is in charge of the Wing, the portion of the prison in which I am confined; that was the first news I had of the death of Oliver Dotson."

Clinton leaned back and waited for his attorney's next question. Walsh could see that Clinton's hands were trembling and a fine film of perspiration covered his face, but Walsh was close to him. The jury and spectators didn't detect any deviation or emotion at all.

Walsh reiterated, "State if at any time or at any time prior to that, you had made any statement to Persinger as to what would be done by James Fleming with relation to the death of your father, as soon as he, McArthur, should be released from the penitentiary."

"No sir," Clinton recited patiently, "we never had any conversation relative to the subject."

Walsh motioned him to elaborate. Clinton spoke slowly, emphasizing his words:

There was never any conversation ever occurred between myself and Ellis Persinger or between myself and Charles Oliver Benson or any other person in which the killing or the death of my father, prior to the 15th of February, was ever discussed, or spoken of, or mentioned in any way. The conversation on the 14th of February was the only time it was ever spoken of, and, before that, nothing was ever said.

Walsh had nothing more to gain by having Clinton repeat the statement. Clinton would only offer a denial. Walsh sensed that wasn't adequate, but knew of nothing else to do.

County Attorney Simpson conducted the cross-examination of the defendant. He strode over to Clinton with a determined air, frowned, and, in a hard voice told Clinton to restate his testimony.

Clinton straightened his shoulders and, meeting Simpson's eyes, repeated his testimony without a pause:

I stated that we were not allowed to talk in the dining room and are never allowed to talk there at any time. Meal times are the only times we are there; at other times the table crew are there.

"What else did you state?"

I stated that I had not had any previous conversation with Ellis Persinger relative to the death of my father, previous to the 15th of February and that I had no conversation previous to that time with James McArthur or Fleming. I never said anything to him about going up to where my father was at all, nor about murdering my father.

A hint of anger could now be detected in Clinton's voice. He continued in a louder tone of voice:

I did not have any conversation with Ellis Persinger in September of last year relative to the same thing, or in relation to our getting out of the penitentiary. I did not state to him in September of last year that we folks would not be in longer than two years as I only saw him twice to talk to while in the prison; that was on Christmas Day and the 14th of February. A month before that, I saw him at a distance but did not get to speak to him. At that time, I was on the wood crew and the first day I was on the crew was the day I was taken sick and did not get out any more and did not get to speak to

Persinger. I did not see him on the 16th of February and was not on the wood crew at that time. McLaughlin was not there. I did not have any conversation with him then. I did not see him another time two or three days later and did not tell him that everything was working all right just as I had planned it.

County Attorney Simpson brought up the previous conviction and Clinton responded:

I remember the time of the death of Eugene Cullinane. At the time I was not really living at one place, but my home was in South Dakota. I was staying in Helena. I know Ed Cachelin; he and I and Oliver Dotson were living in American Gulch. I went into that neighborhood on the 15th day of July 1899, and left there on the 30th of July.

"Why were you arrested?" Simpson demanded.

Before Clinton could respond, his attorney, Walsh, interjected.

"We object to that. I cannot see the relevancy of his arrest on this Cullinane affair. If they open or go into that; we want to subpoena witnesses on our side. It is too remote and is not relevant."

The State withdrew the question, but the jury didn't miss the reminder. Simpson then jogged their memory a bit more.

"I will ask you to state if you know anything about a watch that was found in your mattress at the time of your arrest."

Walsh angrily objected again.

"That is objected to as incompetent, irrelevant and immaterial for any purpose in this case and for the reason that it is not cross-examination."

The court agreed. Judge Clements said:

I don't see how it could be made competent or material to inquire of this witness of these matters. This defendant is charged simply with complicity in this murder while in the penitentiary and as to whether he had anything to do with this alleged confession as it is purported that he instigated it, but, to go into the details surrounding of Eugene Cullinane, I don't see the materiality of it. The objection will be sustained.

Simpson nodded and bent toward Clinton, speaking calmly, "I will ask you to state if you did not have some conversation with James McArthur or Fleming, in reference to the murder of your father and also in reference to a confession that should be found at or near the body of your father after he had been murdered."

"No sir," Clinton answered decisively, "Fleming told me where he was going. He told me he was going to the Bitter Root country, but did not tell me he was going to any place else."

"When did you next hear from him?"

"I received a letter or communication from McArthur after he went out of the penitentiary: I received it on the 15th of February; I am positive it was the 15th of February because the post mark was the 15th when it was delivered here and the post mark was on it when it was mailed."

"How can you be so sure?"

"I generally look at my letter to see how long it lays before I get it. The letter was thrown into the waste bucket: I kept it a week or ten days after I received it."

Simpson then began another line of questioning. His purpose was to bring to the jury's attention evidence that had surfaced in Fleming's trial. Referred to by the press as the "Wyoming Letters," the communications were from Clinton to one Perry Oeschli (pronounced and often referred to in the transcripts as Oxley), and supposedly smuggled out of the prison with Fleming when he was discharged.

In the letters, Clinton had allegedly asked Perry Oeschli, a notorious thief and robber, to come to Montana and murder John Chadwick, John Mulholland or, if that failed, to murder his father, Oliver.

No physical evidence of the letters existed and their content was probably fabricated by Fleming to cast strong suspicion on Clinton. Fleming also contended that Clinton and Oeschli had robbed a train together and hidden the money in Wyoming. It was Clinton's share of this cache that was supposedly allocated to pay Fleming for the murder of Oliver.

Actually, Fleming was the one who wrote to Oeschli and asked for help because he was in trouble after Oliver's murder!

In answer to this inquiry, Clinton said, "I did not give McArthur any letters to take out of the penitentiary with him for me. I have heard of a man by the name of Barry Oxley in Wyoming, but I did not give McArthur any letters to take out of the penitentiary to him."

Simpson dropped the line of questioning, leaving the jury and spectators confused as to the importance of the exchange and continued on another tack. At his question, the jury became alert and listened intently.

"Mr. Dotson, didn't you have a conversation with James McArthur yesterday or the day before, in the presence of Sheriff McMahon, in which conversation you stated to him that you had planned this whole thing to murder your father?"

C. J. Walsh groaned inwardly, cursing the meeting Clinton had with Fleming in the jail. He made an effort, although he recognized its futility, to object on the grounds the question was incompetent, irrelevant, and immaterial. As expected, Judge Clements overruled and ordered the defendant to answer counsel's next question.

"And this conversation," Simpson continued as though he'd not been interrupted, "was had in the County Jail in the Court House yard, and was in the presence of Sheriff McMahon with McArthur or Fleming."

"Well, I cannot tell what was said." Clinton exclaimed.

Judge Clements ordered that the question read again and told Clinton to answer "Yes" or "No" to it.

Clinton listened carefully, then said, "No sir."

Simpson raised his voice "I will ask you to state if McArthur didn't say to you at that time that you knew you planned this whole thing, and you stated 'I did'?"

"No Sir."

"Did he not state to you that you wanted him to kill Chadwick over there and you admitted you had?"

"No sir, there was no such conversation."

Simpson was becoming frustrated and angry. "Didn't you state also at that time that you would go into court and confess the whole business?"

The spectators drew in a collective breath; this was what they had looked forward to–the confession that Clinton was supposed to make. Clinton disappointed them and irritated the County Attorney.

"I said that, if they would allow me to go into court and make a statement, that I would tell the whole thing, all I knew of it. I didn't want to go into the jail but they insisted on it."

"Didn't you state that you would write this thing and tell him you would clear him and that you planned this whole thing?" Simpson persisted.

"I didn't tell him anything of the kind."

Simpson, clearly annoyed by the defendant's contrary answers, continued stubbornly:

After the time of that conversation you had in the presence of McMahon with McArthur, state if McMahon did not ask you if you were going to make that confession, and if you didn't say, 'No, not until after the trial was over as your attorney, Mr. Smith, advised you not to do it?'

Walsh was on his feet, quickly objecting to the question as immaterial. This time the court sustained the defense's objection and instructed the witness to refrain from answering.

Simpson asked some clarifying questions concerning the habits of the prison wood crew, then bluntly and abruptly asked:

At the time you had this conversation with Ellis Persinger on the afternoon of February 24th, I will ask you if you did not make this statement: 'Now Persinger, I have sacrificed my own father and want to get out of here, and you men stay by me or I will turn State's evidence'?

Walsh stridently objected:

Counsel is assuming this conversation took place. It is giving
the jury to understand that they would not remember what the
witness testified to and that he had admitted the conversation
in relation to that subject, and is not whether the conversation
took place between you and he on the 24th of February, or
didn't you or he make that statement.

The wording of the objection was confusing, but the point
was made and Simpson withdrew the question. Walsh asked for
redirect examination. He spaced out his words for emphasis:

State if anything in this conversation, or any part of it with
McArthur in the County Jail, in the presence of McMahon or
any other person, if any statement or admission was made
upon your part; that you knew of or had anything to do with
the killing of your father, Oliver Dotson.

Clinton replied simply, "No sir."
"State if you stated you were going into court to confess you
were guilty of such a charge."
"No sir."
"Was Mr. Smith present at any of these conversations?"
Walsh asked, referring to the defendant's other counsel, Joseph
Smith. Clinton thought for a moment, then replied:

He was the first time I was in there. I was in there twice but I
don't think I was there for over ten minutes at a time. I talked
with McArthur each time I was in there; he was in a cell and
I was in what is termed the corridor inside of the bars. There
was one other present at the time I had the conversation with
McArthur besides the Sheriff, but I did not pay any attention
to who it was. At the time Mr. Smith was in there I was
talking to McArthur.

Walsh asked, "State if the statement was not made here in the courtroom in the presence of the Sheriff, that whenever any conversation took place between you and McArthur, that Mr. Smith should be present to protect you?"

"Yes, sir, but I was put into the cell where Mr. McArthur was during the time my attorney was *not* there."

Satisfied, Walsh ended the questioning and Clinton stepped down.

A considerable difference exists between what should have occurred, and what actually occurred, in the law courts of the frontier west. For the modern accused criminal, a vast network of protective apparatus exists, not the least of which is the Miranda ruling. In 1901, however, confessions were often elicited by whatever means were most effective. During the investigation of Cullinane's murder, the method employed was isolating the suspects and breaking the youngest, most vulnerable member of the trio–Benson.

However, during the second trial, Clinton's story remained intact (supported by witnesses). The officers then turned to another tactic to wrench a confession from him; they forced him into contact with Fleming after Fleming had been found guilty. As expected, a heated exchange occurred. The State was now attempting to use that conversation, unsupported by testimony from Fleming, to either break Clinton on the stand or to convince the jury the incident took place as described. For the most part, the court allowed it and Clinton's attorneys were helpless to do more than protest.

In a surprising move, the defense called Martin Gleason, the prison guard often mentioned during the testimony, to be a witness for the defense. Gleason, obviously ill at ease speaking to the crowded courtroom, testified that he'd been acquainted with Clinton since August 1899 and that the prisoner's conduct was peaceable and tractable. Clinton obeyed the rules and regulations of the penitentiary.

Trippet objected to the testimony because the conduct of the defendant was not material, but Judge Clements overruled him and said he considered the question competent. Gleason then repeated that Clinton's conduct had been good.

The prosecution had no reason to interrupt the next witness. Warden Frank Conley was an impressive figure, even before he began speaking.

He stated that, as warden of the penitentiary, he was aware of the behavior of all the prisoners, and he meted out the punishment for all infractions. He said Dotson was reported once, but the matter was excused. He also affirmed Clinton's statement concerning enforced silence in the dining room.

Walsh and Smith conferred quickly with Clinton, then announced that the defendant, by his Counsel, announced in open court that he rested in the introduction of testimony.

"Was that all?" wondered the spectators. There had been no last minute dramatic confession, no explosion on the witness stand, no new information. Some openly expressed their displeasure and the reporters present looked over their scant notes and experimented with adjectives to attempt to liven up the copy. When the State began its rebuttal, no one was optimistic of any developments. A few people drifted from the courtroom and several women allowed as how they would have to get home to start dinner soon.

W. H. Trippet, for the prosecution, called on Frank Conley who had just settled in his seat. Mr. Conley heaved himself up again and took the stand. Trippet wanted to know about Conley's contact with Persinger.

Conley, rubbing his neck to relieve the weariness he felt in his muscles, stated that he'd conversed with Persinger in the latter part of December relative to what McArthur would do when he got out of the State prison.

"State the general nature of the information he gave you," Trippet said.

Walsh interjected, "It seems to me that this is hardly proper and does not rebut anything brought out in the case and I object to it!"

The judge sustained the objection and Trippet rephrased his question.

"Do you remember sometime last spring when Mr. Simpson, myself, Mr. McMahon and yourself were at the state prison talking to Mr. Persinger?"

"Yes, sir," responded Conley.

"Do you remember whether or not any promises were made to him there relating to a pardon or whether it was refused?"

"There were no promises made him. You told him you would not make him any promises and that there was none to be made. Both you, Mr. Simpson, and I said that."

Only one witness remained for the rebuttal. The State called Sheriff John McMahon. The sheriff documented Conley's testimony concerning no promise of pardon for Persinger, then got to the heart of Trippet's purpose for calling him, asking him if he heard a conversation between Clinton and Fleming.

"I heard the conversation between Clinton Dotson and James McArthur or Fleming yesterday or the day before at the jail here," he said.

No one seemed to find it curious that he couldn't remember which day it was, although he managed to relate the conversation in its entirety.

McArthur said to him, 'Dotson, I want you to state here now, before Sheriff McMahon about this whole matter and I want you to tell the truth in every particular and I also want you to give the names of those parties that you had me carry the letters out of prison for and I want you to go to the County Attorney and my attorney and make a full and complete confession of this affair and asked him if he wanted to have him hanged.'

Dotson made the remark that he did not and McArthur asked Dotson in return if he did not know that he wasn't guilty and Dotson said, 'Yes, I know you are not guilty,' and then gave McArthur the names of two parties whom these letters were sent to by McArthur which he claimed to have mailed at Avon and smuggled out of the penitentiary. He said, 'Dotson, you know you planned this whole scheme and didn't you ask me to go over to Washington Gulch and kill

Chadwick and Mulholland and I told you I wouldn't; that I was a good friend of yours but I wouldn't murder anybody.'

He then asked Dotson if he would go on and make a confession and Dotson said he would. McArthur said, 'Why not do it now?' Dotson said he didn't think he would do it then but said, 'Jim, I will do it tonight, I will make the confession tonight.' McArthur asked if he would have a shorthand reporter to go to the prison with his attorney and make that confession and he said he would.

The next day I asked Dotson if he was going to make the confession and he said he was advised by Mr. Smith to say nothing about the matter until the trial was over, and he refused to see McArthur any more. He said it made him feel bad to see him and I did not put him in there anymore.

The spectators leaned forward, interested again, and listened carefully. C. J. Walsh pounced on his opportunity to cross-examine Sheriff McMahon.

"Did the defendant, at any time, say he had caused the killing of his father?"

McMahon admitted that he hadn't.

Walsh asked, "Dotson did not at any time during this conversation, say in answer to McArthur's question that he had caused the killing of old man Dotson."

McMahon said he hadn't. Still not satisfied, Walsh pressed the sheriff for more information and denial.

"Didn't McArthur stand there and make declarations and this man stood and did not answer except in that part in which he told him he would write the confession?"

"What declarations do you allude to?" McMahon asked.

"I say," Walsh answered clearly, "did not McArthur make all these declarations and this defendant simply stood there and said nothing either one way or the other?"

"McArthur spoke to him in detail as I told it and he answered. He did not answer at any time that he had caused the death of old man Dotson."

Walsh was satisfied and so, apparently, was the State. They rested the introduction of testimony in the rebuttal. The bulk of the trial was over. The courtroom was stifling hot and muggy, and Judge Clements made a reasonable decision: he needed time to prepare his instructions to the jury and they, too, would be in a better state to operate with a night's rest behind them. He adjourned the court until the next morning, Saturday, July 20.

The guards returned Clinton to his cell while a determined Walsh and a resigned, and more experienced, Smith, conversed over the content of the defense's closing statement.

Chapter 25
Verdict
July 20, 1901

On Sunday, July 21, 1901 a special dispatch to *The Anaconda Standard* provided citizens of Anaconda with a detailed description of the closing day of the trial. Most of them knew the major points, either from having been there themselves, or from questioning friends or relatives who had attended. Those few who hadn't heard, read the account avidly. The newspaper observed that, "The closing incident of this eventful trial brought out a large crowd of spectators, of whom many were ladies."

Women *had* flocked to the courthouse that Saturday morning. Shopping was forgotten; bread was unbaked; gardens went unweeded and unwatered. The women of Deer Lodge, out of curiosity, compassion, righteousness, or a need for glamour, crowded onto the benches and waited with hushed voices.

When Clinton entered the courtroom, feminine fragrances, violet toilet water the most predominant, assailed him. The female scents, mixed and mingled, struck him so forcibly he felt lightheaded. He hadn't smelled much except his own sweat and the rank cell for months. He saw that many women in the crowded room were short, plump, and plain like his wife, Mary. He was glad Mary wasn't in the courtroom, glad she couldn't afford the long trek from South Dakota to Montana. As much as he missed her, needed her, he couldn't bear for her to see him like this.

Clinton tensed as the women turned to observe him; he fought to keep his expression impassive, but he felt a sharp pain in his stomach and his heart was racing. He shivered. Although the July heat was building, he felt chilled and shrunken. He tried to shrug off the fear. The best thing to do was avoid looking at anyone. He walked deliberately and swiftly to his chair at the defense's long oak table.

The prosecution opened with their final remarks. Clinton's attorneys looked weary. Joseph Smith sat quietly, but Walsh repeatedly went through his papers, seeming to pay scant attention to the prosecution presenting their arguments. Clinton sat still and silent as usual, but his eyes were wary and constantly moving over the faces of the jury.

W. H. Trippet opened the argument for the State. His address was directed along much the same line as it was in the McArthur trial. When he referred to the prevalence of crime and to what the citizens of this county were expecting from the jury, he was interrupted by Attorney Walsh, who came out of the intense perusal of his notes and sprang to his feet at Trippet's words, which were exactly what he'd been fighting all along in the trial. As far as he was concerned, Clinton was being tried again for the Cullinane murder and all the other acts of criminal violence the people of Montana had suffered.

Walsh didn't think his client had a chance, although the prosecution's only evidence was the testimony of a convict and the details of Fleming's crime. Now he angrily protested. The court agreed, and sustained Walsh's objection. Judge Clements instructed the prosecution to refrain from any mention of prevalence of crime as it was out of place.

The jury had, however, been duly reminded of what was expected of them. Mr. Trippet spoke for forty minutes and cited many telling points for the prosecution. He dwelt at length upon the great number of peculiar circumstances that had been combined to show that Dotson and McArthur were the guilty parties.

He was followed by Joseph C. Smith for the defense, who spoke for almost half an hour and found many flaws in the State's evidence. He insisted that the jury shouldn't condemn a man to death upon the sole testimony of a convicted murderer (referring to Persinger). He asked them to give the same weight to the testimony of the prisoners who testified in Dotson's behalf (and who came forth in greater numbers) as they did to Persinger's testimony. Mr. Smith held that the entire charge against Dotson hung by the slender thread of evidence proffered by Persinger's account. This, he claimed, had been refuted by testimony just as good, and just as reliable, as the testimony of Persinger, who had hopes of a pardon.

Smith's defense was valid and might have swayed a less emotional, more sophisticated jury, but these were simple, hardworking men who were fed up with lawlessness. They also, no doubt, found it hard to disclaim the tall, open-featured, good-looking Persinger, who came from solid Missouri farming stock, in favor of the scruffy prisoners who had come to Clinton's defense. After all, some might reason, wasn't one of them serving eighty years–a life sentence–for murder? It was easy to overlook the fact that Ellis Persinger, too, was a convicted murderer. He'd only gotten a ten-year sentence. That must mean the evidence wasn't too strong against him.

Smith gave it his best. His argument, deserving of more consideration than it received, was sound but seemed ill-received.

The recess for noontime refreshment came early and was abbreviated; Judge Clements had a busy schedule planned for that day. Clinton didn't get lunch at all–the jail staff had been unprepared for the short break. He did get a cup of warmed over coffee and briefly smoked his pipe; he didn't think he could eat anyway.

After the break, C. J. Walsh had his turn to argue for the defense. Walsh began his argument on behalf of the defendant and for almost an hour held the close attention of the jury, as well as that of the spectators. He went into the testimony very minutely, at one point referring to the fact that Mr. Glover of Avon and Mr. Conley of the penitentiary had differed materially about the time when McArthur left the prison. Mr. Conley saying he left late in the evening of December 30 and Mr. Glover saying he (McArthur) had eaten dinner at his hotel at Avon on December 30. This, Mr. Walsh held, only went to show how easy it is for people to be mistaken in dates. He hoped to show how superficial much of the evidence put forth by the prosecution was when subjected to close examination. Finally, he asked the jury to give the case the same consideration they would were the best citizen of the community on trial. He closed with a powerful appeal for his client, and asked that the jury render a verdict of "not guilty."

Walsh had been concise, persuasive, and passionate in his plea. He believed in the inherent value of the legal system and argued not only for his client, but for the fine letter of the law. His reasonable and learned discourse might have been highly effective on an urban jury who approached their decision from a hypothetical viewpoint; however, he was speaking to men who walked the same streets and drank in the same saloons as the criminal element of the small mining towns—men who were vulnerable to, or often victims of, various unlawful acts.

Another brief recess was granted for the prosecution to prepare their closing statement.

When the court reconvened at 1:30 p.m., County Attorney J. M. Simpson began the closing argument by saying that Dotson had planned and caused to be perpetrated the most heinous crime that has ever been committed in the state; he was interrupted once by Mr. Walsh, who objected to him going outside the evidence.

Clinton heard someone in the back of the courtroom say the temperature had reached 96 degrees. The jurors fidgeted and twisted in their seats as they fanned themselves. Many wore their best—and possibly only—suit, and were suffering in the heavy, dark clothing.

One man after another ran his finger under his tight collar and loosened his necktie. Even the attorneys unbuttoned their jackets. Clinton watched as their shirt collars became limp with perspiration, but he didn't feel the heat. He was too intent on what the judge was saying.

He listened as the judge gave the jury instructions. As each word fell from the judge's lips, his attention grew more marked, especially when the judge explained the different degrees of murder and the attendant punishments.

At 2:30 p.m., the case went to the jury, and the twelve men retired to consider the evidence. At 3:30 p.m., a scant hour later, a verdict had been reached. The defense team no doubt realized that the sweltering conditions inside the courthouse would hasten the jury's decision. It did; the jury deliberated a scant forty minutes, although it took another twenty minutes to write out the verdict and wait for the judge to return to the courtroom. There was but one ballot taken, and the verdict was unanimous for conviction of murder in the first degree

WE, THE JURY, FIND THE DEFENDANT, CLINTON DOTSON, GUILTY OF MURDER IN THE FIRST DEGREE.

Clinton was stunned. Listening to his attorneys make their closing argument, he was convinced they would persuade the jury of his innocence, or at least the lack of hard evidence. The afternoon assumed a dreamlike quality for him as he dealt with the reality of their decision. He shook his head and looked at Walsh for confirmation. Walsh nodded sadly and whispered to Clinton that they could always try for an appeal. Clinton sat frozen; he was the only person in the courtroom oblivious to the suffocating heat.

When polled, each juror answered that such was his verdict. The judge discharged the exhausted jury members and adjourned the court until five o'clock. Judge Clements had pressing business in Helena, and wanted to finish the entire business quickly; therefore, sentencing would be the same day.

As Clinton exited the congested courtroom, a comely, well-dressed woman spoke to him and he answered her. As he moved on, the woman's friend grasped her arm and said,

"What did he say, tell me? Did you tell him we felt sorry for him?"

The other woman looked at her friend with a perplexed frown. "Yes," I told him, "we ladies want to say that we feel awfully sorry for you. Then he said, 'It's too late for sympathy now.'"

"Is that all?" demanded her companion.

"Yes," she said, "except he called me the oddest name, he called me 'Old Girl.'"

The other woman giggled and agreed it was an odd thing to say. They pushed their way from the courtroom to take some fresh air and a stroll before the sentencing at five o'clock.

Clinton was unaware he'd called the woman one of his pet names for his wife. All the way to his cell the words kept running through his mind in a crazy, singsong patter. "Too late now, too late now, too late now."

The Anaconda Standard reported:

When the hour for reconvening of the court arrived the courtroom was crowded with those who had come to hear sentence pronounced upon Dotson. Many had crowded inside the bar to watch Dotson and see if they could discern any trace of emotion in his features. But they were disappointed. Dotson stood like a statue and listened to Judge Clements.

The judge cleared his throat and passed his hand across his sweating brow. The temperature had been rising steadily all day, and now the body heat generated from the crowd in the room made it so stifling he could hardly draw a full breath. He looked at the prisoner in front of him, attired in a dark jacket and trousers and wondered why he wasn't sweating also. He hurried on with his task.

Mr. Dotson, you may stand up. The county attorney of the county, on the sixteenth day of April, filed in the court an information charging you with the crime of murder in the first degree, in killing of Oliver Dotson on the fifteenth day of last February. To that information you pleaded 'Not Guilty.'

You have been tried by a jury of twelve men and found guilty of murder in the first degree. Have you anything to say why the judgment of the court should not be entered, or any legal reason to present?

Clinton raised his head and looked at the judge; his voice was very low as he replied.

"I do not know as it would benefit me to say anything."

Attorney C. J. Walsh announced that the defense had no legal reasons to urge why sentence shouldn't be pronounced. The spectators in the court strained forward as the judge leaned toward the defendant and spoke in somber tones; expecting the jury's verdict, he'd prepared the speech the night before.

I think, Mr. Dotson, that you have had a fair trial, and I believe that everything that was possible for attorneys to do has been done in your behalf by the attorneys who defended you. So far as my conduct is concerned I have endeavored to be impartial, and if I have committed any errors in my conduct and in my rulings it has been in your favor and against the State. I think you must be conscious of the fact that you are a desperate man, and I trust that you will meet the fate that you have brought upon yourself with the same feeling which is characteristic of your life. I am also of the opinion that you are responsible for getting James Fleming into the trouble that he is now in. I think Mr. Fleming is a man capable of committing any crime, but after having committed it he is as helpless as a child to protect himself, and it has brought both you and him to the trial and conviction.

He paused for a moment and looked down at the papers before him, then at the stiff figure of the man in front of him. Clinton displayed no signs of emotion, but he was deadly pale and his eyes looked back at the judge with a blank expression, as flat and gray as slate. Judge Clements spoke slowly and clearly.

The judgment of the law and the sentence of the court is that you be remanded to the custody of the sheriff of the county and on the 6th day of next September you be, by the then acting sheriff of the county, hanged by the neck until you are dead.

On July 21, 1901, *The Anaconda Standard* in its Sunday edition, reported the activity following the announcement.

When the court had finished Dotson conferred for a moment with his attorneys and then started with Sheriff McMahon for the jail, where he will remain hereafter.

Penitentiary Doesn't Want Him –

Dotson desires to be sent back to the penitentiary to await his execution, but he has been remanded to the custody of the sheriff and will occupy a cell separate from that of McArthur in the county jail. Col. Tom McTague said, in speaking of Dotson's desire to return to the prison: 'We do not want Dotson, even though we should get $10 per day for keeping him. His presence at the prison would have a most undesirable effect on the other prisoners were he there.' Attorneys Walsh and Smith have filed notices of intention to move for a new trial for both McArthur and Dotson. An order of the court was asked and granted to have the court stenographer prepare a transcript of the evidence in order that a bill of exceptions may be made. Thirty days, in addition to the statutory time, was allowed in which to prepare the motion for a new trial. Court stenographer McGuinness says that a copy of the evidence in the two cases will comprise about 1,000 folios.

When the hangman's noose is extended, ready to encircle their necks on Friday, September 6, James

Fleming and Clinton Dotson, in the little town of Deer Lodge–within the walls of the county jail–come, on this Sunday morning, to a full realization of the enormity of the crime they have committed and of the terrible retribution that has overtaken them.

People read the paper that morning and nodded. Yes, a double hanging would be a grand spectacle and a strong deterrent to those who challenged justice in the newly formed county of Powell, Montana.

Part Three

The Executions

Chapter 26
Fleming Dies
September 6, 1901

As July wound down, Clinton's attorneys were busy requesting a new trial and the newspapers were milking the case for all it was worth.

On July 20, Clinton's attorneys filed a notice of an intention to move for a new trial. They based their request on an "insufficiency of evidence" and "errors of law occurring during the trial." The next day, the Sunday edition of *The Anaconda Standard* had reported, in a special editorial, that the "State's new county has set a new pace," and "has made an example out of Dotson and Fleming."

The publicity wasn't necessary; by July 25, the officials received hundreds of applications for cards of admission to the execution. It became an arduous task for the sheriff to sort through and decide who would receive invitations.

While Clinton was adjusting to his new cell in the city jail, Mary had received copies of the newspapers and now knew the worst. For once, the grinding exhaustion of taking care of the children, providing for them, and keeping their small homestead operating was a blessing for her. She simply had too little time to dwell on it during the day; it was at night, alone in the old double bed, when she ached for Clinton. Often, she would go into the other room and bring her youngest daughter or one of the twins back to bed with her, seeking comfort in the warmth of their bodies until she could sleep.

The oldest boys were aware, as was the eldest daughter, that their father was to hang, and they vowed to try to save him. When Mary heard, she not only wrote to the Montana governor, begging him to spare Clinton's life, but asked friends and relatives in Spearfish, South Dakota to write in supplication. Thus began a letter writing campaign–pleading for his life–that continued until the day of his death.

In the meantime, Clinton's moods swung like a pendulum. Some days, the jailer noted, Clinton seemed to be very calm, almost content, as he passed the time fixing up his cell and smoking his pipe. Other times, he was anxious and demanding, wanting to know if his attorneys had been in or if any news had arrived on his motion for a new trial. Reporters and visitors, some from a considerable distance away, thronged around the jail, hoping to catch a glimpse of Fleming or Dotson. Clinton could only wait, ignoring the scrutiny.

On August 21, *The Silver State* reported that Fleming's lawyers had refused to appeal his case. That left no doubt in anyone's mind but that the ugly, red-haired killer would be hanged on September 6 as scheduled.

On the same day Fleming's attorneys abandoned him, Clinton's attorneys concluded that they did, indeed, have grounds to request a new trial for Clinton. The news buoyed up Clinton immensely, and, on August 26 they told him they had filed a bill of exemption and a motion for a new trial. Two days later, they wrote to the governor of Montana asking for a sixty-day respite so that a motion could be heard: the governor granted the request and gave the lawyers until October 25.

The printers had already prepared the invitations for a double hanging. They contained captioned pictures of James Fleming and Clinton Dotson and read:

Mr._____
You are invited to witness the execution of James Fleming (alias James McArthur) and Clinton Dotson on Friday, September 6, 1901, at 10 o'clock a.m., at the Powell County jail, in Deer Lodge, Montana.

They were signed by the sheriff of Powell County and considered a coveted prize. Even when it became obvious that only one man would hang on September 6, requests for the permits to the execution accelerated daily. Not since the street fair and carnival, held in Butte on July 14, had such a festive air prevailed.

Clinton expressed concern for Fleming, but underlying the empathy was a strong surge of renewed hope for his own case. Surely, he reasoned, if the governor had granted the respite until late October, he must believe that Clinton's guilt wasn't fully established. Perhaps a new jury would believe him innocent. Clinton clung to the new prospect while attempting to ignore the bedlam surrounding Fleming's execution.

It was impossible, however, to shut out the flurry of activity surrounding the jail. Reporters and the curious swarmed around the yard, asking dozens of questions of the guards and carpenters building the scaffolding. What kind of rope would be used? What style of gallows were they building? How long would it take for the death to occur?

Clinton couldn't shut out their voices, or the sound of the hammers striking nails into the wood of the new, 75 x 75 foot enclosure where the gallows would be erected.

Fleming was becoming desperate as the day drew near. On August 29, he told reporters of *The Anaconda Standard* that Oliver Dotson had told an ex-convict in Helena a few days before his death that he was "tired of living" and that his son, Clinton, had been falsely imprisoned for the murder of Eugene Cullinane.

In another interview, two days later, he said that the publicity of *The Anaconda Standard* "had hurt him considerably," but that he would "forgive all." That same day, he was soothed by a group of tenderhearted ladies who brought him homemade ice cream, cake, and a bundle of late summer flowers for his cell.

By September 3, Sheriff McMahon had mailed out three hundred invitations to the execution: the amount requested had been over double that figure.

Fleming was so agitated by September 5 that he attempted to commit suicide. Clinton alerted Sheriff McMahon that a woman, sympathetic to their pitiful prisoner, had smuggled a surgeon's probe and passed it to Fleming. The sheriff received Clinton's note in time to stop Fleming from completing the act, although he was bleeding from a severed artery. A twenty-four-hour watch was instigated for the rest of the day–extending until the time of execution the next morning.

On the night of September 5, Fleming decided he wanted to die a Catholic. He requested and received baptism. The guards said they would miss him; he was an exceptionally good story teller and had entertained them for hours.

The next morning, September 6, was a foul day, cold and gloomy. Still, over 200 spectators turned out to witness the execution. Many inmates and guards at the jail expected Fleming to be carried, kicking and screaming, to the gallows, particularly in view of his aborted and frantic attempts to convince listeners of his innocence in the days preceding the execution. Surprisingly, Fleming seemed to find a strength of character previously not apparent. He chose to die bravely. Drawing himself erect, he spoke to the assembled crowd:

Gentlemen,
I am here to meet my death. I have been brought to this unjustly. I have been bought and sold like a beast. I hope that the officers now here will be able sometime to find and catch the parties who are guilty of the crime for which I have to suffer death. Perhaps they will have to meet the same fate. I forgive all who have wronged me, and I ask forgiveness of all. I want to state, standing here on this green turf, that I am sincerely in earnest when I tell you that I am an innocent man. I can meet my Maker in Heaven innocently. I thank you all for your attention. I am ready now to meet my Maker. Thank you.

The 3/8 inch woven hemp rope was adjusted around his neck and carefully tightened in against the dark hood. At the signal, a 312 pound weight was released. It dropped three feet. Fleming rose and, according to *The Silver State*, was "jerked into eternity" at 10:17 a.m.

A reporter for *The Silver State* also noted that Fleming was buried the same afternoon–the interment witnessed by Sheriff McMahon, Father Phelan and "the dead man's two brothers." Other sources indicated that none of his family was there to say goodbye, if indeed any existed. At the time he entered the penitentiary he listed no names or addresses for relatives. It was recorded that his birthplace was Milwaukee, Wisconsin.

The Anaconda Standard reported the next day that Clinton was very visibly affected when Fleming was taken away the previous morning; that he'd cried and pleaded with Fleming, begging him for forgiveness, but that Fleming wouldn't grant it. Clinton had reportedly prostrated himself before Fleming, so distraught was he that the man would die without forgiving him.

In a statement to *The Anaconda Standard*, however, Clinton simply said, after being told that Fleming was dead,

Of course my feelings are hurt by the knowledge that he is dead. I know that he is innocent. I know that he should not have been executed. But, he died bravely. He died happy. He had no fear of the gallows and went to his death as an innocent man should.

More of the story concerning Clinton and Fleming's behavior during their last encounter might have surfaced had not the newspapers a much larger event to cover. The day after the execution, the news was broadcast that, on the same day James Fleming was hanged, a twenty-eight year old anarchist, named Leon Czolgosz, unemployed, despondent, and disenfranchised from society, walked into a public reception at the Pan-American Exposition in Buffalo, New York, and fired two shots into President William McKinley's chest and stomach.

For the next seven days, the newspapers across the nation would carry little else on their front pages. McKinley was treated at the site and a press release said that he was slated to recover. However, due to a variety or problems surrounding the medical treatment–including the doctor's inability to locate one bullet and an improperly sewn and drained incision–McKinley developed gangrene and was pronounced dead on the evening of September 14 by his attending physician. The twenty-fifth president of the United States had suffered for a week before succumbing to the infection.

Theodore Roosevelt was his successor and political events pre-empted the local news for the rest of September.

Chapter 27
Clinton Appeals
September 18, 1901 to March 26, 1902

With reason to hope, Clinton settled into his daily life in the jail without protest. Even at the penitentiary, he'd been a tractable prisoner, now he continued to be little trouble for the jail guards or sheriff. He spent long hours smoking his pipe and working out plans in his head for ways to help Mary if he was sent back to the penitentiary. He wouldn't allow himself to think that his appeal might be denied.

Before his last trial, he fashioned a particularly handsome bridle, made of black and white horsehair. He worked the slogan "Rough Riders" across the front headstall. He sent it to Mary, and she wrote that she wouldn't auction it off unless his execution was canceled. She wanted it as a memento, a tangible proof of her husband's work over the last few years. As Clinton sat in his cell and meditated for long hours, he planned how to acquire materials to make similar bridles; with Theodore Roosevelt now president, the ones referring to Roosevelt's "Rough Riders" would command a better price at a raffle. The plain ones he sent the boys had brought a fair amount. Maybe he could help Mary and the children after all.

The nights were harder. Often Clinton would wake in the quiet hours between midnight and dawn and feel dread course through his entire body; at those times he abandoned all hope and had to force himself to get out of his cot and pace his cell until he could banish the apprehension.

C. J. Walsh and Joseph Smith, deciding that Clinton's case was worth the time and effort, had followed their filing of an intention to move for a new trial with a formal motion for a new trial which they filed on September 18, 1901, twelve days after Fleming's execution. An order of reprieve was granted by the Honorable J. K. Toole, Governor of the state of Montana, and delivered to Sheriff John McMahon: the execution was postponed until April 4, 1902, pending the outcome of the appeal for a new trial.

After careful consideration, the two attorneys concluded that a motion for a retrial was feasible based on several errors and discrepancies. In a prepared document, they stated their objections were based on lack of evidence in that:

Specifications wherein the evidence is insufficient to support the verdict of the jury and the judgment of the court.

Because the verdict of the jury is against the law in this. That there is no evidence to show that the defendant was accessory before the fact.

Because there is no evidence to show that the defendant advised James Fleming to commit the crime charged in the information.

Because the only testimony introduced upon the trial of said cause showing or tending to show that a crime was committed is in the evidence connecting the said James Fleming with the said crime.

Because there is no competent evidence to show the deceased came to his death in the manner and form charged in the information (see testimony of Dr. Dodd's in transcript).

They listed eight errors in law occurring at the trial and excepted to by the defendant. They listed three cases in which the court erred in permitting witnesses to answer questions over the objections of the defendant's counsel. They noted that the court had erred in refusing to give the jury the instruction that,

To authorize a conviction upon circumstantial evidence alone, the circumstances must not only be in harmony with the guilt of the accused, but they must be of such a character that they cannot reasonably be true in the ordinary nature of things, and the defendant be innocent.

The court also erred, according to Walsh and Smith, in refusing to instruct the jury that,

In order to justify the inference of legal guilt, from circumstantial evidence, the existence of the inculpatory facts must be absolutely incompatible with the innocence of the accused upon any rational theory, and incapable of explanation upon any other reasonable hypothesis than that of his guilt.

Additionally, the court did not tell the jurors that,

The rule of law is, that to warrant a conviction on a criminal charge upon circumstantial evidence alone, the circumstances should be such as to produce nearly the same degree of certainty as that which arises from direct testimony, and sufficient to exclude all reasonable doubt of the defendant's guilt. The circumstances ought to be of such a nature as not to be reasonably accounted for on the supposition of the defendant's innocence, but be perfectly reconcilable with the supposition of his guilt.

The court instructs the jury, that as an invariable rule of law, that to warrant a conviction for a criminal offense upon circumstantial evidence alone such a state of facts and circumstances must be shown as that they are all consistent with the guilt of the party charged, and such that they cannot, upon any reasonable theory, be true and the party charged be innocent.

Lastly, Clinton's attorneys pointed out that proof must exist in harmony with the circumstantial evidence to convict a defendant.

It was a good argument, and one that should have occurred to anyone who was following the case intellectually rather than emotionally. Perhaps cooler weather and a less publicized trial would have rendered longer, more thoughtful deliberation.

As it was, the jury convicted Clinton without a shred of physical evidence; he was condemned to death on the word of a convict who could only gain from the cooperation he extended to prison officials–if not a pardon or preferential treatment, then certainly the sweet reward of revenge against the man whom he insisted had plunged him into his present circumstances.

Clinton's attorneys settled back to wait for word on the appeal for a new trial. Word wouldn't come until late February.

Christmas, 1901 was a joyless one for Mary and her brood. It had been a particularly hard winter with the snow coming early and covering much of the gazing land that supported her milk cows and hogs. She'd been forced to buy feed for them much earlier than anticipated, and she worried that her money would run out long before spring. That Christmas Eve, she and the children sat quietly in front of the old cook stove in the kitchen, listening to the wind howl around the eves of the log house.

They drank coffee and ate bread sweetened with brown sugar and spread with *schmierkase*. She also distributed their Christmas presents; each child received a penny for every year of their age. In all, Mary handed out less than a dollar, but each of Clinton's children, even his oldest son, now sixteen, thanked her warmly. She took comfort in the fact that she'd thus far kept her family together without any outside help at all.

Clinton partook of a much heartier Christmas dinner than did his family. He spent the afternoon watching the snow drift down past his cell window and wondering how Mary was faring. The next two months were cold, dismal, and agonizing for him. The waiting for news seemed interminable.

Clinton found himself feeling both relieved and disappointed at the end of each day in January and February. If the news–when it finally came–was bad, then the longer it took, the better; each day was one more day of life. On the other hand, if he were successful in his appeal, it would be a tremendous load off his mind; he could return to the penitentiary and hope of a pardon.

When word finally did come, it was devastating. Sheriff McMahon went into Clinton's cell on February 25 and told him that he wouldn't get a new trial and that the execution, pending official notification, would probably be carried out as scheduled on April 4. Stunned, Clinton and broke down and wept openly in front of the officer; it was one of the few times he allowed his emotions to be seen publicly.

The guards moved him to a different cell and gave him an entire change of clothing to make sure he didn't "cheat the gallows." The guards watched him closely. The next day, Clinton seemed to reject the inevitable and told his jail attendants that he still doubted he would ever hang. He said he expected to get a life sentence when he went before the judge for re-sentencing. He even told them, in detail, how he planned to fix up his cell in the penitentiary when he returned. They listened, but continued to keep a close watch on him. He asked to have a picture made of him for Mary. That request suggested that, at least subconsciously, he considered that his death was possible.

On March 26, 1902, *The Silver State* reported that Judge J. M. Clements had, on Monday, March 24, 1902 formally re-sentenced Clinton Dotson to hang on April 4. Clinton, the paper said, did "not wince" at the news and, when returned to his jail cell, calmly lighted his pipe.

The same paper had published an article on March 19th detailing a statement Clinton purportedly gave to Rev. Dr. A. B. Martin, in the hope it would be passed on to Gov. Toole and result in clemency. In it, Clinton blamed Persinger and his nephew for Cullinane's murder. He also spoke of a bizarre plan McArthur devised to kill Warden Conley, stage a jailbreak, and get Benson, Persinger, and one other man out of prison. Clinton then described how McArthur (Fleming) hatched yet another plan that would achieve the same end–the release of Persinger and Benson.

. . . Dotson said, McArthur planned the Washington Gulch murder, telling him about it, and asked him who he could kill over there suspicioned of the Cullinane murder. He expected to kill the man and place the confession of that killing on his victim. Getting no satisfaction out of him, Dotson says McArthur, some time after, told him he and Persinger had agreed that he, McArthur, when he got out of prison, would murder old Chadwick and place the confession on him.

The day before McArthur left the prison, however, Dotson says the former and Persinger got together and switched the victim from Chadwick to his old father, Oliver. Clinton says McArthur told him all about it two days before McArthur was hanged. He said Persinger urged it because he thought the confession would go further because his father (Clinton's father, Oliver) had no friends in the neighborhood. Says Dotson: The people wonder who killed Cullinane in American Gulch, I will tell you who done it, and it will no longer be a mystery. It was Ellis Persinger and Oliver Benson. Persinger told me so, and he told his lawyer so. He said they went there to rob him and he made fight and was about to strike Benson with a pick when he shot and Benson shot at the same time. He said they had no intention of killing him when they first went there–not till he made fight and had to. He said that Benson got ten dollars off him and he (Persinger) got his watch and they didn't go near his horse.

The statement made interesting reading, but affected neither the officials nor the public who were eager to see Clinton hang– both for the spectacle and for the comfort of knowing a dangerous criminal would be eliminated.

Clinton's oldest daughter traveled to Montana to beg the governor for clemency. She prostrated herself on the steps to his residence, but was never received.

Governor Toole also received pleas and letters from a number of women asking that mercy be extended to Dotson. To some, Clinton had become a cause, and they implored the governor to commute Clinton's sentence to life.

On April 2, *The Silver State* reported, "Governor Toole today received from Joseph Smith letters from Mary Dotson . . . and other friends in Spearfish, South Dakota, asking for executive clemency."

The next day, April 3, the paper carried the news that Governor Toole, at three o'clock that afternoon, had denied appeal and wouldn't commute the sentence to life.

The Anaconda Standard, in their morning edition on April 4, said that Joseph Smith, the condemned man's attorney, had broken the news as gently as possible. Clinton's last hope was shattered. Smith told Clinton he'd talked with Toole at Missoula and the governor said he could see no reason why he should interfere in the decree of death. That while he felt great sympathy for the relatives and friends of Dotson, he could not consistently consider their pleading on behalf of the condemned man.

The Anaconda Standard went on to report that Clinton had reacted strongly to the news the previous day.

Dotson was half sitting, half reclining on his bunk when he heard the words of his faithful attorney. He was toying nervously with a more than half-consumed and lighted cigar. He could not speak. Twice he tried to, but his voice failed him. He realized that several pairs of eyes were intently watching him and made a great and partially successful effort to regain his composure. Several times he puffed vigorously at his cigar, rolled it back and forth in his trembling fingers and then abandoned it to pick up his handkerchief from his knee and twist it nervously about his fingers.

When Dotson had concluded talking he shed a few tears. Then he grew morose and sullen and declined to talk until several hours later when he sent for Sheriff McMahon, the Reverend A. B. Martin, his chief spiritual

advisor, and Deputy Warden John A. Robinson of the penitentiary, who arrested Dotson for the murder of Eugene Cullinane in 1899. To each he made unimportant statements, and assured all that he forgave them for anything they might have done against him.

The newspapers carried on a running debate over whether one of Clinton's statements constituted a "confession."

The Anaconda Standard of April 4 believed it did. They said that Clinton Dotson "with death staring him in the face, admits that he was a conspirator in the plot which had its object the murder of his aged father." They then printed the alleged confession which they called "unexpected" and "sensational." Next to the boxed statement was a photographic collage consisting of a picture of the gallows, the last picture of Clinton, taken in his cell on March 29, a photograph of the invitation to his execution, and a picture of the Deer Lodge Courthouse. The text of the alleged *confession* read:

I know I have no chance now, and I am ready to die. This is hard, because I have not been a murderer in fact. I did conspire with McArthur, Benson, and Persinger to have my father killed, but later, when I thought it over, I washed my hands of the deal. I had previously been a party to the conspiracy to kill John Chadwick, but that plan fell through.

After I had refused to have further connection with the conspiracy to kill my father, Benson and Persinger went right on with their plans. I saw them many times in the yard of the penitentiary in earnest conversation, and I knew they were determined upon a consummation of the scheme. I was in honor bound not to betray them, and could say nothing until it was too late. I would have said nothing even then regarding my oath to them as sacred, but for the fact my father's life was at stake. It was a case of either my father's death or that of Warden Conley.[1.]

The moment I received the letter from McArthur I knew my father was dead. The rest was easy for Benson and Persinger. They framed up their story to show my guilt, and my word would not be taken against theirs. That is one particular thing I regret about my conviction, and I think it is not just. I was found guilty on the testimony of convicts.

I know you have done everything for me, Mr. Smith, and I appreciate it. It is all over now and I am reconciled. I will go out tomorrow morning and do the best I can to be brave. It will not be hard to meet death, but to face the crowd that will gaze upon me. That will be about the only thing that might make me weaken. I know from experience, because all the stamina was taken out of me on the 24th of last month, when I faced the crowd in the courtroom to receive final sentence. I do not think I have been treated right by the courts or by the newspapers, but I forgive everybody and bear no person any enmity.

It will be an awful disgrace to my family for me to hang. I have no fear of death. If it were not for my family, I would prefer to hang than be imprisoned for life.

The Anaconda Standard reported that the statement was made by the "condemned man with a perceptible effort. His voice trembled and choked, his eyes dimmed with tears, and his hands tugged nervously at his straggling gray beard and mustache alternately."

The Butte Miner, in their Saturday morning edition on April 5, disagreed,

In spite of stories of a "confession," nothing of the sort was obtained from Dotson by anyone. He said nothing in addition to what he had already testified to in his letter to the governor. He was talkative . . . but did not give to anyone a confession of his guilt. When it came to the point where his connection with the affair was concerned he was as mum as the proverbial oyster.

On the evening of April 3, after learning his plea was denied, Clinton appeared calmer–he seemed to have collected his thoughts and braced up. His statement to Joseph Smith wasn't a confession as such, but more of an effort to tell Smith that he appreciated the lawyer's effort and to assure the lawyer that he, Clinton, hadn't misrepresented himself or his actions.

Clinton spoke with various people who came to his cell, including Warden Conley. Conley, hoping to clear up an area of confusion, asked Clinton if he'd spent a term in a Wyoming prison.[2]

Clinton said there were several men named Clinton in the Dotson family, and the incident had involved one of the others, not him. The reporter for **The Butte Miner** noted that Clinton became angry when he realized that his statement wasn't believed and appeared "much relieved when Mr. Conley left the jail."

During the evening Clinton talked freely with those who came, particularly his guards. At one point, he spoke of his emotions. "The worst part of all this has passed with me now. I have made up my mind and shall not worry anymore."

Of the clergy, he said, "I have kindly feeling toward all churches. Reverend Martin is an old man . . . I have especial confidence in him . . . he has been a great help to me, and I expect him to be with me at the last."

Reverend Martin agreed to go to the scaffold with Clinton. Previously, the Catholic priest said he couldn't accompany Clinton to the gallows unless Clinton embraced the Catholic faith. Clinton decided that he wouldn't embrace Catholicism as it might mean he would be interred in the Catholic burial ground where Fleming had been laid to rest.

Early in the evening, when he offered a drink, he said, "Whiskey? No, I have none and I do not care for it. I never did like the taste of it, and it would not do me any good now. I could have all I want, but I have not taken a bit."

As the hours wore on, Clinton received yet more company. The sheriff's daughters, Misses May and Nellie McMahon, took a cake and a generous portion of sherbet to him. He was pleased and expressed his gratefulness to them. He then sent for Sheriff McMahon and asked him for forgiveness, in that he'd misjudged him and "entertained a wrong impression" of him. Momentarily regaining some of his spirit, Clinton informed the sheriff that he had a knife concealed where he could easily get at it and that if he wanted to do so, he could take his own life and cheat the gallows. He then told them if he was manacled, which had been suggested, he could remove the irons with little trouble. He told the sheriff just how he could do it.

Throughout the evening, Clinton seemed to fluctuate between solemn statements and defiant claims, from philosophic acceptance to bitter denial.

Chapter 28
Clinton Dies
April 4, 1902

Clinton's cell became crowded as the night wore on. *The Anaconda Standard, The Butte Miner,* and *The Inter Mountain* had all sent special reporters to Deer Lodge on Thursday morning's train. They, with the reporters from *The Silver State,* various law officers, and Reverend Martin were with Clinton in his cell, off and on, until nearly 4:00 a.m. on April 4. The reporters and officials plied him with questions, hoping he would make admissions or furnish information about the crimes. A reporter from *The Silver State* said,

For the first time since his incarceration he drank freely of liquor, and his tongue loosened up considerable under its influence, but he was yet guarded and failed to make a confession, which the reporters had counted on getting.

The two guards assigned to the death watch, Charles Aspling and Undersheriff Dee, along with Sheriff McMahon, were surprised at how well Clinton bore himself. Although they thought he was artificially courageous, they had to admit that he faced the ordeal calmly, at times indifferently. They had expected a complete breakdown and were amazed at his self-possession.

His consumption of liquor was the only irregularity in his behavior. He asked for, and consumed at frequent intervals, a mixture of whiskey and port wine. As he drank, he talked willingly with his guards, and only displayed strong emotion when shown the photograph of himself that he requested. It took several moments for him to regain control, then he thanked them and asked that they mail it to his wife and family.

At 4:00 a.m. he ate a light meal, then, drowsy from the food and alcohol, took to his bunk, requesting they call him early so he could receive Sisters of Mercy, Hilaria and Bertina, whom he wanted to see before his execution. However, he slept heavily and, when the two women came, according to their promise, he couldn't be aroused. The guards awakened him finally at 10:45 a.m.

Meanwhile, the citizens of Deer Lodge had been stirring for hours. April 4 was a glorious day; the sun shone brightly and the air was clear and balmy. By seven o'clock, the streets of the town were "showing signs of unusual life" according to a reporter for *The Butte Miner*.

People were about the hotels and saloons talking of the coming event and speculating on the behavior of the principal in the performance. Little groups soon formed on corners and everywhere there was talk of nothing but the event of the day. Many were the stories circulated of the probable outcome of the morning's program, and rumors of improbable things. The story to the effect that Dotson had confessed was greeted with the acceptance it deserved and no one believed it for a moment . . . some sheepishly admitted that they had been victims of sensationalism and tried to make their listeners believe that they never half-believed in the story anyway. The bright sunlight of the early morning felt good and seemed to take away the solemnity which everyone knew was due the day.

At midmorning, word passed from group to group that the execution would be postponed until later than originally scheduled. No trains ran into Deer Lodge the night before and many people, who wanted to come from Butte, were disappointed. They were coming in on Friday morning's train instead and Chief of Police Reynolds and Sheriff Furey, along with other prominent officials, asked

Sheriff McMahon to postpone the hanging until the train from Butte arrived. He agreed to do so. In keeping with the festive air surrounding the jail, the prison band gave a concert to entertain the visitors while they waited for the execution.

When the train from Butte pulled into the station, approximately two hundred people piled off and hurried to the scene of the hanging. Many crowded into the corridor of the building housing the jail. *The Butte Miner* reported,

It was all the good-natured officers could do to keep them from wanting to tear down the walls in order to get a glimpse of the chief actor in the morning's drama.

The gates leading into the stockade were opened soon after the crowd arrived at the jail and it was only when the visitors were led to believe that they would get but a poor chance to see the hanging if they did not hurry for the enclosure that the main building was cleared. People wanted to see the principal in one of the most dastardly crimes ever committed in the West go to his end . . . wanted to see Dotson meet his doom.

Law officers flocked to the execution as well. In attendance were Warden Frank Conley; Deputy John A. Robinson; Sheriff Savage from Miles City; Sheriff Jack Conley; Deputy Joe Daly; Deputy Sheriffs Pelletier and McGavey from Butte; Chief of Police Reynolds; Policemen Sullivan, Byrne and Hines from Butte; Former Chief of Police Jack Lavell from Butte; Game Warden Will F. Scott from Helena; Deputy Warden Henry Avare from Butte; Deputy Sheriff T. J. Hanifen from Helmsville.

If Clinton heard the prison band's lively music, or the good natured murmuring of the crowd of over 500 people, he gave no sign of it. When Reverend Thomas H. Phelan gently roused him, Clinton groaned and pulled himself upright. They offered him food, but he declined roughly, saying he wanted nothing more than a cup of coffee. He drank it as Sheriff McMahon helped him dress. He put on clean linen, a new black suit, a white shirt and a black tie. Clinton was nervous and kept shedding tears while making his toilet. At one point, he seemed to gain control of himself and braced up while neatly brushing his hair. Then he sank again into a chair and wept for several minutes.

Reverend Martin tried his best to console Clinton and seemed to have his attention. Clinton sat quietly listening to the church man, only occasionally sobbing. He was still seated when Sheriff McMahon read the death warrant, although Clinton seemed too preoccupied to take any notice. Reverend Martin took a Bible from Clinton's cot and read a passage that seemed to comfort the condemned man.

After a few minutes of prayer, Sheriff McMahon told Clinton to stand up so that straps might be applied and adjusted. As his arms were bound, he tried several times to speak but was unable.

Finally, in a quivering tone, he asked for liquor. A tin cup, nearly full of the whiskey and port wine mixture he'd consumed so freely the night before, was held to his lips. He drained the entire cup and didn't utter another sound as he was led to the gallows.

As he stood on the scaffolding, looking at the crowd, he held himself stiffly and silently. At 11:27 a.m. Sheriff McMahon adjusted the noose around Clinton's neck and put the leg and waist straps in place.

One lone man, in a crowd of over five hundred people, felt the need to say goodbye to Clinton. His voice rang out over the hushed assembly. "Farewell, Clint."

At 11:29 a.m., the heavy, 312 pound weight dropped. Clinton's last and only words were "Catch hold of me, I am going to fall."

A reporter for *The Anaconda Standard* described the execution with passion.

There was scarcely a perceptible tremor as Dotson's body settled at the end of the rope. Drs. J. H. Ownings

and E. F. Dodds stepped forward immediately and each grasped a wrist, feeling for the pulse. They stated at 11:37, that there was no pulse and 15 minutes later announced that the heart had ceased to beat. The neck, they said, had been broken, and they were sure that death was instantaneous.

It was the first time in the annals of Montana and possibly elsewhere that a convicted murderer, who had been sentenced to serve 99 years in a penitentiary, was legally executed for a second murder. It was the execution of a brute at heart, an apathetic to a marked degree and a coward who affected a stoicism which he was able to maintain to the end, except for a brief interval, and which created with many the impression that the patricide accessory before the fact died "game."

The Butte Miner was more convinced of Clinton's bravery, but no less dramatic.

Clinton Dotson, the unnatural son who planned the death of his father in order to get himself out of the penitentiary . . . was hanged today without giving out a word as to his guilt or innocence. He died game and never said a word to the crowd.

Additionally, they reported,

It was a gruesome sound to hear the baying of a hound shortly after Dotson had been sent on his way to eternity. The dog was evidently just outside the stockade surrounding the scaffold and as soon as the rope holding the weight had been cut, the animal began to moan and cry like a man wounded to the death and crying in his agony for assistance. Many spoke of it and several who were superstitiously inclined explained the meaning of the bad omen.

A reporter for *The Anaconda Standard* was more poetic:

Dotson Spoke of Birds

But at the same time, the day was bright and not one on which to die. It was hard for the man who knew the fate soon to overcome him and fully as difficult was it for the sworn officer of the state to do his duty while everything in life seemed so sweet.

Many times had Dotson spoken of the birds in the trees outside his prison house and expressed the hope that he might see them sometime and listen to their singing as a man without a care and free from stain of the law's conviction. There were nests outside the jail and they are there now. The robins and swallows had been building their homes in the limbs of the pines there and their music as they went about their happy tasks sounded to the saddened prisoner like the singing of angels. He even went as far as to express the belief that he would hear them again sometime and gave a sign of hidden sentiment which he did not exhibit to everyone.

The Butte Miner reported that the execution was one of the most successful ever carried out in the state of Montana.

Afterword

Although with every decade, every century, every millennium, we see scientific, cultural, and societal changes throughout the world, it seems individual human behavior stays strangely static.

In Plato's *Apology,* he speaks of the trial of Socrates in Athens in 399 B.C.E. Plato portrays Socrates as telling the crowd that he was convicted due to his reluctance to say what others expected.

> You think that I was convicted through deficiency of words–I mean, that if I had thought fit to leave nothing undone, nothing unsaid, I might have gained an acquittal. Not so; the deficiency which led to my conviction was not of words–certainly not. But I had not the boldness or impudence or inclination to address you as you would have liked me to address you, weeping and wailing and lamenting, and saying and doing many things which you have been accustomed to hear from others, and which, as I say, are unworthy of me.

There is no way to know if Socrates uttered those words, or if Plato only wished he had; however, should Plato's work be based on fact, perhaps Clinton, like Socrates, might have benefited from a more emotional defense.

End Notes

1. Clinton was referring to a scheme he revealed to a reporter on *The Silver State* on March 19, 1902, in which he said McArthur planned to kill Warden Conley with hopes that a change in management would lead to confusion and an escape could be effected.

2. Conley was going on information given to him by Deputy Warden John A. Robinson, who said Clinton told him he'd been sentenced for murder four years ago, but that since the murder was a case of self-defense, the term of imprisonment was only one year. Clinton's last surviving son, Jesse Dotson, recalled that his father supposedly served one year in the Wyoming penitentiary at Rawlins for killing a man who was trying to rob him and his partner (in an ambush of their wagon) of their mining profit (gold dust) near Chugwater, Wyoming. To further confuse the issue, Clinton did have an uncle named Clinton. He also had two cousins named Clinton–one whose birth date is unrecorded; the other who was fourteen years Clinton's junior.

Additional Notes:

Although similar, records indicate Oliver Dotson's wife, Sarah, spelled her maiden name Flemings, as opposed to Fleming. Records do not suggest any relationship between her and James Fleming (aka James McArthur).

The full text of Clinton Dotson's appeal, and the court's rejection of that appeal can be found as:

Report of Cases Argued and Determined in the Supreme Court of Montana, Volume 26, State v. Dotson, published by Bancroft-Whitney Company, 1903.

Epilogue

Clinton was executed two days before his and Mary's eighteenth wedding anniversary. He was buried in Deer Lodge, Montana. *The Silver State* reported, "The remains were taken to the J.M. Bien undertaking rooms, from where next morning the undertaker, Sheriff McMahon, Dr. Martin and Sexton J.G. Foster accompanied them to the cemetery, where interment was made in the grounds set apart for the convict dead." None of Clinton's family was present; they had neither the heart nor the means to attend.

Persinger did not get a pardon, and served the six years required (for a ten-year sentence); he was released on June 18, 1906. Benson served his full sentence; he was released on January 12, 1906.

Mary did receive the photo of Clinton, taken just six days before his execution. In it, he is seated, his hands clasped loosely in his lap. His hair is neatly combed and his full beard, appears white. His gray eyes gaze out at her as steady and unwavering as ever.

Mary moved her large family to a ranch nine miles north of Sturgis, South Dakota, in 1903. There, two miles west of the famous Bear Butte, she homesteaded and dry farmed. She continued to raise pigs, chickens, and keep a few cows to help feed the family. Mary became a neighborhood midwife and, during the influenza epidemic in 1918–when three out of five persons afflicted died–stayed healthy and nursed her neighbors.

Her son, Jesse, said that after Clinton's death, Mary had opportunities to remarry, but refused all, even in the face of her poverty. She said she could never love anyone but Clinton, and would not take a chance on marrying a man who might abuse her children.

Gradually, as her nine children left home, Mary became financially stable. She sold the ranch in 1927 and, after living for a time in Denver, Colorado, moved to Casper, Wyoming where she lived with her daughter. She died on May 3, 1932. Her last words were remarkably similar to Clinton's: "Hold me," she cried.

All of Clinton's children stayed in touch and lived productive and successful lives. Only his youngest daughter did not live to old age–she died during surgery at age 54. His youngest son was the last to die, in April 1985, just short of his eighty-ninth birthday.

Shortly after Clinton's second trial, Oliver Dotson's .38 caliber Winchester rifle and a well-worn, double-barreled shotgun were sold at an administrator's sale in front of the courthouse. Undersheriff Dee got both for $2.00.

Of the fate of Dan and Dick, the team of horses much loved by Clinton's children, no record exists.

The horsehair and silver bridle that Mary kept, in the event Clinton was executed, has survived in good condition.

Oliver is buried alongside his wife, Sarah, at Rosehill Cemetery in Spearfish, South Dakota.

Deputy Warden John Robinson, whose career seemed to advance along with Clinton's misfortunes, was beaten and stabbed to death on March 8, 1908 during the first major escape attempt at the penitentiary. Two of the four convicts attempting freedom attacked Robinson and Warden Conley. Robinson's jugular vein was severed and he died. Conley was also severely wounded, requiring 103 stitches to patch him together, but survived. The two prisoners, wounded by Conley, recovered but were both subsequently hanged for the crime.

The Montana Territorial Prison functioned from 1871 until 1979. Frank Conley was warden from 1890 to 1921. Conley turned a deteriorating prison into a viable facility through an ambitious building program using inmate labor. The convicts were also involved in various work release programs, not the least of which was road building, logging, and ranching. Conley also served as mayor of Deer Lodge, Montana.

Clinton's great-nephew, Jack Frandsen, became interested in researching Captain Oliver Dotson's life. We both hoped his research would turn up a photo of Oliver, but so far none have surfaced. What he did find, however, were items in the Deadwood, South Dakota newspaper archives in which Clinton Dotson was mentioned. Not all the articles were positive: Clinton was before the local court on several minor charges. One notable court appearance put Clinton before the same judge, in the same courtroom, and at the same time that Harry Longabaugh (aka Sundance Kid) was sentenced to 18 months. Whatever Clinton's case involved, it appears to have been deferred or dismissed.

On a more positive note, it was reported Clinton received a contract from the county commissioners for the care of the county paupers, and had moved them, bed and bedding, to comfortable quarters on upper Sherman Street. Clinton is also mentioned as catering supplies to the Lawrence County Poorhouse near Central City.

Several years ago, I met Irene P. Lambert, a highly respected graphologist who was certified in 1985, and became a master graphologist in 1992. For the last several years, she has operating her business under the name I.P. Lambert, LLC. Among other services, Ms. Lambert offers Genealogical Personality Analysis for a study of family history. Since I had a lengthy letter in Clinton's hand, as well as his signature on his wedding certificate, I submitted the material to Ms. Lambert for her opinion. I gave her no background information, other than to point out he'd been convicted of two murders–which had occurred over 100 years ago.

Interestingly, her comments concerning Clinton's demeanor seemed to echo what various newspaper reporters had said. One particular area, in her analysis of his personality structure, described traits that may have contributed to his undoing. Ms. Lambert said:

Clinton was more of an introvert, holding people at his distance and going with his own council. He had an uncomfortable concern about the impression he was making upon others, especially people he did not know. This made him even more uncomfortable in unfamiliar situations with unfamiliar people.

Things that concerned him personally were often rationalized, making him reluctant to recognize the facts. Since it is impossible to determine whether or not a writer committed murder, the focus becomes the structure of the personality of the writer. Usually when someone commits an aggressive crime, there are many hostile traits within the writing as well as anger. This was not the case for Clinton. The handwriting was not from a hostile individual, but more of a strong-willed one.

Clinton was an emotionally responsive person, and his feelings influenced his decisions. While he could act impulsively in some situations, his sense of personal worth would have curbed extremely negative reactions.

Newspapers:

The Anaconda Standard
August 16, 1899
August 17, 1899
August 18, 1899
August 19, 1899
August 25, 1899
August 29, 1899
August 30, 1899
September 5, 1899
September 10, 1899
September 17, 1899
October 5, 1899
October 6, 1899
October 7, 1899
October 8, 1899
October 9, 1899
October 10, 1899
October 11, 1899
October 12, 1899
October 13, 1899
October 14, 1899
July 20, 1901
July 21, 1901
August 29, 1901
August 31, 1901
September 7, 1901
April 4, 1902
April 5, 1902

The Silver State
October 11, 1899
October 18, 1899
February 27, 1901
July 17, 1901
July 19, 1901
July 20, 1901
July 24, 1901
August 21, 1901
August 28, 1901
March 19, 1902
March 26, 1902
April 2, 1902
April 3, 1902
April 9, 1902

The Butte Miner
April 5, 1902

Documents:

Photocopies of original court documents obtained from Clerk of Court, Powell County, Montana, and Clerk of the District Court, Anaconda, Deer Lodge, Montana, October 1982.

Trial One: Eugene Cullinane's Murder

Documents from of the District Court of the Third Judicial District, of the state of Montana, In and for Deer Lodge County:

August 11,1899: Arrest Warrant issued by State of Montana, County of Deer Lodge, and signed by Frank Kennedy, Justice of Peace for Oliver Dotson, C. O. Benson, and John Doe (Oliver crossed out and Clinton substituted; John Doe crossed out and Ellis Persinger substituted).

August 15, 1899: Handwritten inventory of possessions found on Dotson, Persinger, and Benson at time of arrest, including description of Eugene Cullinane's watch. Unsigned but on stationery from Sheriff's Office, Deer Lodge County, Anaconda, Montana, Jack Conley, Sheriff.

August 16, 1899: Statement made by Charles Oliver Benson in the County Jail in the Sheriff's Office.

October 2, 1899: Subpoena for Witnesses for the first trial.

October 10, 1899: Document confirming Clinton Dotson's Conviction of Murder in the Second Degree

October 12, 1899: Document issuing order of incarceration and a sentence of ninety-nine years at hard labor for Clinton Dotson in the penitentiary at Deer Lodge, Montana.

October 21,1899: Notice granting Attorneys Trippet and Self until December 11, 1899 to file motion for new trial.

November 21, 1899: Affidavit from John W. Jameson regarding Ellis Persinger's advising Charles Benson not to testify.

November 21, 1899: Document asking for a continuance for Ellis Persinger's trial.

November 23, 1899: Order for Clinton Dotson to be furnished a transcript of trial–reference murder of Eugene Cullinane.

December 9, 1899: Notice for extending time to prepare a bill of exceptions for a new trial until January 20, 1899.

March 7, 1900: Notice to Attorneys Trippet and Self that the notice of intention for a new trial was not served within the time allotted.

Trial Two: Oliver Dotson's Murder

Trial documents (photocopies and/or transcribed hand copies) from existing records of Powell County, October 1982.

April 14, 1901: Order for arraignment on murder charge (Dotson and Fleming).

April 16, 1901: Document ordering Clinton Dotson confined to the State Prison at Deer Lodge, Montana as a convict and Frank Conley and Thomas McTague as the contractors for his keep.

April 16, 1901: Order for Conley and McTague (State Prison at Deer Lodge) to produce defendant Dotson in court for the arraignment.

July 13, 1901: Jury Finding James Fleming Guilty of Murder in the First Degree, signed by Foreman of Jury, Earnest P. Schumaker.

July 17-20, 1901: Trial transcript (their pages numbered 18-168) containing testimony of Clinton Dotson's trial for complicity in murder of Oliver Dotson. Contains testimony of all witnesses.

July 20, 1901: Jury Finding Clinton Dotson Guilty of First Degree Murder, signed by Foreman of Jury, Ben D. Lear.

July 20, 1901: Document remanding Dotson to custody of Sheriff of Powell County (after conviction of First Degree Murder).

July 20, 1901: Appeals document.

July 20, 1901: Document requesting copy of stenographic notes as defendant Fleming was without means.

July 20, 1901: Notice of Intention to move for new trial– defendant Fleming.

July 20, 1901: Document requesting copy of stenographic notes as defendant Dotson was without means.

July 20, 1901: Notice of Intention to move for new trial– defendant Dotson.

August 26, 1901: Notice of Intention to move for new trial for Dotson (complete statement with service notations).

September 19, 1901: Motion for new trial, defendant Dotson.

April 5, 1902: Notice of compliance with execution of Clinton Dotson on April 4, 1902, signed by John McMahon, Sheriff.

Books:

Dotson, James M. And Wilson, Barr. *Richard Dotson (1752-1847) and his Descendants*. Danville, California: Published by James M. Dotson, 1992.

Havighurst, Walter. *Voices on the River*. New York: The Macmillan Company, 1964.

Wolle, Muriel. *Montana Pay Dirt: A Guide to the Mining Camps of the Treasure State*. Denver, Colorado: Sage Books, 1963.

Time Life Editors and O'Neil, Paul, text. *The Rivermen, The Old West Series*: Time, 1975.

Photocopied Documents:

The Anaconda Standard
September 5, 1899, morning edition.
Artist drawing of Sheriff Jack Conley, Deputy Sheriff, John Robinson, Ellis Persinger, Clinton Dotson, and the wagon in which they were captured.

The Anaconda Standard
July 21, 1901.
Artist's drawing of courtroom scene, captioned: *Attorney Walsh Making His Final Plea and Ridiculing the Theory of the State As To How the Shot Was Fired*.

The Anaconda Standard,
April 4, 1902, morning edition.
Photo of Clinton Dotson (the photograph made for Mary prior to execution), captioned: *Latest Photo of Clinton Dotson*
Photograph of gallows, captioned: *The Gallows*.
Photograph of invitation to execution made out to Mr. Anaconda Standard and captioned: *Invitation to Execution*.
Photograph of Deer Lodge Courthouse captioned: *Deer Lodge Courthouse showing High board enclosure in the rear*.

The Anaconda Standard,
April 5, 1902, morning edition.
Artist's drawing of Clinton being escorted to gallows, captioned: *Clinton Dotson's March to the Gallows*.
Inset drawing captioned: *The Man Who Bade Dotson Farewell*.

The Butte Miner

April 5, 1902, morning, second edition.

Photograph of Clinton on the gallows captioned: *Murderer Dotson's Life Was Taken on Gallows in Twinkling Of An Eye*.

Photograph of courthouse captioned: *Courthouse In Which Dotson Was Convicted of Foul Crime*

Additional Documents

Original Copies:

Marriage Certificate for Clinton Dotson and Mary Blake, indicating they were married on April 4, 1884, Dakota Territory.

Handwritten letter from Clinton Dotson (in prison) to Mary, dated April 7, 1901.

Two pages from a bible sent to Clinton Dotson's son, (R) Dotson, by Conley & McTague, wardens at the Penitentiary at Deer Lodge, received at the post office in Whitewood, South Dakota, on March 24, 1900. The bible is in German—it apparently belonged to Mary who spoke German. The two pages recorded Mary Dotson's (nee Blake) birth as well as that of her siblings. It is unknown why Clinton would have it with him, and why the wardens at the prison would send it to his youngest son, although Clinton may have requested they do so.

Letters dated May 10 and May 25, 1982, from the Office of the Warden, Montana State Prison, Deer Lodge, Montana, answering my initial inquiries.

Newspaper clipping from scrapbook of Jesse O. Dotson (Clinton's son), from Deadwood, South Dakota newspaper, date unknown but approximately September or October 1934.

Six page record written by Jesse O. Dotson (Clinton's youngest son) in 1969, entitled *Mother, Mary Blake Dotson*.

Old Montana Territorial Prison brochure with brief history (including chronology) and describing Frank Conley's tenure as warden.

INDEX OF INDIVIDUALS

Others:

Annet, William–42

Arnold, S. N.–29, 129, 161-2

Ashley, H.H.–42

Bacon–114

Benson, Charles, Senior. (m. Virginia Dotson)–32

Benson, Charles (Clinton's nephew)–5-8, 14, 16-28, 32, 40-42, 47, 51, 55, 59-63, 66, 69-72, 76, 130-32, 136, 140, 144, 105-1, 172, 174-8, 181, 183, 198, 205, 232, 234-5, 256, 252-3

Berry, Minor–134-5, 166, 174, 179

Bien, M.–47, 132, 172, 246

Bradshaw, J.–147

Bush, S. C.–125, 126

Cachelin, Edward–16-7, 42, 44, 130, 149, 200

Cardon–185-6

Chadwick, John–14, 15, 16, 25, 40, 42, 201, 203, 208, 232, 234

Chapman, John D.–71

Christoffersen, Frank–44

Church, C.–147

Clancy, James–110

Colbath, C. H.–42

Cullinane, Eugene–7, 9-11, 13-17, 20-1, 39-41, 47-49, 52-3, 56-58, 63-66, 69,70, 72, 76, 113, 129, 132-3, 136, 145, 149, 171, 172, 176, 184, 197, 200-1, 205, 211, 232, 234, 252-3.

Custer, General–33

Czolgosz, Leon–225

Dana, W.–147

Davis, Levi–157, 158

Davis, Allan–126

Dengler, William, Sr.–44

Dodds, Dr. E. F.–172-3, 242

Dotson, Hiram–132, 137

Dotson, Jesse–28-9, 78, 103, 245, 247, 257

Originally from Wyoming, Jennie L. Brown is the award winning author of *Blue Moon Rising: Kentucky Women in Transition.* She is a frequent speaker, and presents workshops on oral history. Her short fiction and essays have won honors in various competitions. She is a Professor Emerita at Western Kentucky University. Although she now lives in Kentucky, her heart remains in the West.

Made in the USA
Lexington, KY
04 April 2011